Handbook

for an

Integrated Life

Handbook

for an

Integrated Life

A PRACTICAL GUIDE TO
ALIGNING YOUR EVERYDAY CHOICES
WITH YOUR INTERNAL COMPASS

Sharon Schneider

GREENLEAF
BOOK GROUP PRESS

Published by Greenleaf Book Group Press
Austin, Texas
www.gbgpress.com

Distributed by Greenleaf Book Group

For ordering information or special discounts for bulk purchases, please contact Greenleaf Book Group at PO Box 91869, Austin, TX 78709, 512.891.6100.

Design and composition by Greenleaf Book Group and Mimi Bark
Cover design by Greenleaf Book Group and Mimi Bark
Cover images used under license from ©Shutterstock.com/Artos; ©Shutterstock .com/Vinko93; ©Shutterstock.com/Salim Nasirov; ©Shutterstock.com/VoodooDot; ©Shutterstock.com/musicman

Publisher's Cataloging-in-Publication data is available.

Print ISBN: 978-1-62634-935-3

eBook ISBN: 978-1-62634-936-0

Part of the Tree Neutral® program, which offsets the number of trees consumed in the production and printing of this book by taking proactive steps, such as planting trees in direct proportion to the number of trees used: www.treeneutral.com

TreeNeutral®

Printed in the United States of America on acid-free paper

22 23 24 25 26 27   10 9 8 7 6 5 4 3 2 1

First Edition

To my husband, Bill, who has made it possible for me to pursue my dreams of an integrated life by providing the kind of unwavering support every woman needs and deserves

To my kids, Audrey, Charlie, and Willa, who inspire me to work toward a world worthy of their gifts and passions

To my parents, Jim and Rosalie, who taught me many of the principles that I try to give voice to in these pages

Contents

Contents

Introduction

I'm not doing this to save the world. I'm doing it to save myself.

I come from a family that was stable, loving, and hardworking and valued my education. We volunteered regularly, preparing meals and delivering them to homeless shelters and building houses with Habitat for Humanity. I was a Girl Scout and played every possible sport. My dad coached a bunch of my teams, sometimes assisted by my mom, and they were all terrible, but that was normal and no big deal.

Life in those early years was quite siloed: I was raised in the Catholic faith, but religion was kept separate from work. Volunteering was about showing compassion, not filling in the gaps of government policy. What we had for dinner came in boxes and cans from the grocery store, sort of like money comes from ATMs. How did it get to the grocery store? No idea. I also have no idea who my parents voted for; it didn't seem important.

I just knew that my Grandma Sturtevant yelled at the TV when Reagan was on. Sometimes she chucked her slipper at him to make a point.

When I got to college, however, I discovered that everyone else had not necessarily grown up in such a supportive atmosphere, rich with opportunity and encouragement to follow their dreams. I had not only financial assets like a scholarship and a car but the self-confidence to talk to adults like a peer, even argue with the professors in my small honors seminars. I had (and still have) the open heart and easy laugh of a well-loved kid who had been told she was smart and special—and believed it.

But I met many people who didn't fit that description, people of different sizes, shapes, races and ethnicities, nationalities, different levels of financial security and physical ability. The observation of these differences attached itself to my Catholic instinct to fight for social justice—and the more I realized that others didn't start with all my advantages, the more I felt compelled to try to level the playing field.

There's a saying I love: "Born on third base, thinks he hit a triple." It's the worst insult I can throw at someone. Which is why I say I was born on third base and *know* I didn't hit a triple. I know I started out with a lot of advantages, and I think a lot about how I can use my advantages to help others.

I'm now a middle-aged white American woman with a college degree and a solid career, happily married for twenty-one years, with three healthy kids, two rotten dogs, and a very nice house in Denver. I'm considered an expert in using strategic philanthropy and impact investing to make a difference in the lives of others.

I've been a staff member and a consultant for some of the largest foundations in the world, and dozens of much smaller ones. I help companies integrate social impact into every facet of their operations, from how they treat employees to how they source materials and select vendors, to their environmental efforts and charitable giving. My professional life is about making an impact at scale.

At the level of the individual, though, how do we make an impact? It feels like there is a raging debate between the people saying, "Don't use plastic straws; they're bad for the environment" and those saying, "Plastic straws aren't the problem here; only governments can address the real environmental issues." So who's right, and how should we respond in the face of problems that are bigger than any individual's ability to fix them? I decided that I might not be able to solve the problems myself, but that doesn't mean I should make them any worse if I can help it.

Striving for Shared Prosperity

My whole life, I've tried to be a good person. I don't cut people off in traffic, I return my shopping cart to the designated spot, I forgo the aforementioned plastic straws when given the opportunity.

But what does being a "good person" even mean? For me, at the most fundamental level it means embracing *shared prosperity* instead of lopsided benefits for me and my inner circle of family, friends, and those who share my political ideology.

Yet many unseen and unquestioned forces in American culture work against shared prosperity. What was once touted as the American Dream was reinterpreted as "rugged individualism" and somehow mutated into "every man for himself." As an American, you are encouraged to "get yours" first and then think about others. Friends and experts alike urge us to make our money, secure our future, find our fame. Follow these clever #lifehacks to get ahead of your contemporaries, get over on the system, get access to exclusive events and opportunities. And then, in your encore career or second act, you can give back some portion of your riches. And don't worry about the individuals who haven't managed to find success; it's their own fault for not working hard enough, not having gotten enough education, not creating a vision board in order to manifest their destiny.

On second thought, the forces that shove these "me first" messages down our throats aren't really unseen; those messages are plastered all over social media, movies, songs, TV shows, and ads. People who successfully work the system and achieve great personal wealth are celebrated as geniuses and visionaries. They represent the ideal of "American success" that we should all strive to achieve, or so we are told.

Working against those norms, trying to make life choices that give others a chance at winning alongside us, isn't easy. It requires more creativity, more humility, and more willingness to leave something on the table. Could you save a few bucks by tipping 15 percent on your tab before taxes, instead of 25 percent on the after-tax amount, as the CNBC article "This Simple Tipping Trick Could Save You over $400 a Year" suggests?[1] Sure, I guess. I just can't get excited about that kind of advice on how to be smart. Maximizing every transaction and every relationship to benefit me personally feels like a short-term win but a long-term loss.

The Pandemic Changed Perspectives

In my life, I want my family to be happy and healthy—doesn't everyone? But I also want the people who make our clothes, grow our food, improve our homes, deliver our packages, teach our kids, protect our communities, and otherwise serve society to be happy and healthy too—that support should be a two-way street. In 2020, we came to call these people "essential workers." And as a nation, we realized how interdependent we are. Each one of us needs the person next to us, or across from us, or before us, or behind us to be mentally and physically healthy for society to function in any meaningful way.

The pandemic has prompted Americans of all ages to turn inward, rejecting the quest for material belongings in favor of the search for meaning. We're quitting our soul-killing jobs. We're moving to the places we truly want to live. We're prioritizing our well-being over climbing someone else's stupid ladder. Instead of treating philanthropy as a holiday check-writing exercise divorced from the rest of our lives, many of us are striving to integrate our personal passions, professional expertise, consumer habits, vacation time, and even our household buying decisions into a single identity that expresses a consistent set of values.

I'm no longer content to compartmentalize my life, working to fund good causes during the week and then spending my weekends buying fast fashion from the manufacturers who create the very conditions of despair that I'm fighting against. Globalization, with all its complications, has made us aware of the impact of our actions, buying habits, and lifestyle on people half the world away. And awareness brings a new urgency for action.

Creating a Compass, Not a Road Map

I truly believe we want to do the right thing, but most of us aren't sure what the right thing is. To tell you the truth, I'm not always sure either. Sometimes I find out that something I thought was beneficial is actually causing problems. Like renting clothes by mail, which I've done on and off for years as a way to avoid buying new work clothes every few months (and which I mention later in the chapter about clothing). Now I find that a recent study by a Finnish team found that, because of the frequent dry cleaning and shipping, remote rental services have a higher environmental impact than simply throwing clothes away.[2] Ouch. Okay, so no more clothing rental services for me.

The changing landscape of options, of new knowledge or newly available services means that there is no perfect set of rules, and there never will be. Sort of how nutrition advice has changed over the years as we learn more. Fat went from being the super-villain to the helpful sidekick, and coffee and red wine are back in the "healthy" category, which is good because I was going to drink them either way. Our mental models must change as we learn and grow.

This book, then, is not intended to be a road map with turn-by-turn directions telling you all the things you should and shouldn't do. What we believe is helpful today may turn out to be harmful when we learn more tomorrow. And there are so many challenges in front of us, so many issues we might be passionate about: climate change, the gender pay gap, racial trauma, gentrification, the mistreatment of animals, public corruption, just to name a few. It's seldom easy to find choices that lead to clear positive impact on all these different aspects of our personal and global lives.

Instead, I'm hoping to share my own internal compass, the way I find my "true north" when I'm not sure how to proceed. I call that true north an *integrated life*.

What Is an Integrated Life?

We don't always connect the words "integrity" and "integrated," but they are both saying something about wholeness and consistency.

Someone with integrity stands by their words, backing them up with action. They have the same principles in public as they do when no one is looking. They are consistent. This quality of being whole, and consistent, is what an integrated life is about. It's about understanding that your values aren't compartmentalized, just like your life isn't compartmentalized. We no longer want to separate "making money" from "making the world better" or separate our personal lives from our work lives. We don't want to be one person in real life and an edited and polished (and unrealistic) version of ourselves on social media. We want to work for socially responsible companies and buy organic and fair trade products. We want our role models to be good actors and athletes and leaders and also good human beings. We want our homes to be comfortable and fashionable and also energy efficient. We want our cars to be high-tech and well designed and not contribute to greenhouse gas emissions.

In short, we want to express a consistent set of values in every part of our lives. We want to take what has become splintered and make it whole. Taking the fundamental value of shared prosperity and applying it to every facet of our lives—that's an integrated life.

Be Better, Not Perfect

There is a scene from the NBC sitcom *The Good Place* that explains how humans are scored on every action, and at the end of their lives, they either end up in heaven ("the Good Place") or hell ("the Bad Place") based on their cumulative score. But, as one immortal character explains, human life is so complicated that you can't always anticipate the consequences of even the simplest actions:

> These days just buying a tomato at a grocery store means you are unwittingly supporting toxic pesticides, exploiting labor, contributing to global warming. Humans think that they are making one choice, but they're actually making dozens of choices they don't even know they are making.[3]

When you don't know the consequences of your actions, how can you make choices that are aligned with your values? You can't. And in some ways, you aren't supposed to.

The Good Place is actually saying that the game is rigged because the game is invisible. Sometimes it does feel like that when you live in American consumer culture. If you are just doing what everyone else seems to be doing and what movies, TV shows, social media, celebrities, and other culture keepers tell you, then the consequences are often invisible.

So am I here to tell you we're all going to the Bad Place? No. First, I don't believe in the Bad Place, so there's that (sorry, Sister Anne!). But I'm actually not here to bring you down—I'm here to empower you. I think the corporate culture wants you to feel helpless, to feel inconsequential, to feel like it's impossible to change the way things are, and why should you try so hard, anyway?

I'm actually here to tell you the opposite—that you are far more powerful than you realize. To tell you that you do in fact have choices and that those choices can be less harmful, more helpful, and, most importantly, more in line with your values and intentions. I'm here to empower you to live an integrated life.

As an American, the environmental impact is high and the social benefit of our lifestyle is pretty low compared to many parts of the world. I am not planning to move to a remote terrain and grow my own food and make my own candles and clothes and walk everywhere. That said, there is a *long* way to go from our standard American lifestyle to living an integrated life. So I continually work at getting better but don't beat myself up for not attaining perfection. I prefer Starbucks coffee to local places, so I go to Starbucks. I drive less and walk more, but I'm not selling my car (although it is a hybrid). In short, I try to be better, not perfect.

That's why you won't find recipes for perfection in this book. Instead, Part I lays out seven principles that I've found helpful in guiding me to make better decisions. Part II provides action tips for how you can turn the principles into small or large changes in how you live your life every day.

BABY STEPS, BABY STEPS

As you read through this book and think about your own life and what you care about, it's easy to get overwhelmed by the huge number of possible life changes competing for our time and attention. Overwhelmed enough that you might be tempted to decide it's just not possible to make a difference and give up. So my advice to all of us who simply want to do better is "think baby steps." And my challenge: Pick that one issue and really adopt it and follow through on it in every aspect of your life. Don't try to tackle everything all at once—it's too much. Whichever one speaks to you the loudest, ignites your outrage and your passion—pick that one, and live it. Let your choices every day be part of the solution.

I've come to a point in my life where I don't want to be pulling with all my strength just to try to get some kind of forward movement. I want to help create a world where others are pulling in the same direction with me, whether in an organization, a team, an office, or a community. I want to be aligned, to be joyously working toward the same vision of a more just world. One where we can live our values in every aspect of our life—in the clothes we wear, in the food we eat, in the entertainment we consume, in the way we earn a living, move around our community, and interact with our neighbors.

There are some aspects of American culture that have rubbed off on me, and I can't quite shake them—the fear of being labeled a "communist," sure, but also the need to save for my kids' college education and for my own retirement, to build a nest egg for me and my family (in other words, to "get mine"). But in writing this book, I hope to shake off that scarcity mindset, to *be brave*, and to live authentically. I hope that together we can find the courage to make individual and collective choices about the world we want to live in and to bring that world to life. If you feel the same way, I hope you'll keep reading.

PART I

Seven Principles for Leading an Integrated Life

Every day, each of us faces hundreds of decisions. What we eat. What we wear. How we move from place to place. Where we work. How we celebrate and recreate. How we spend our time and our money. How we behave toward our loved ones, coworkers, and strangers.

Now layer on the desire to make sure that more of these decisions are consistent with an integrated life, and the result can be exhausting. Scientists talk about how "decision fatigue" can happen in the course of a single day; now imagine over the course of a week, a month, or years on end!

That's why I find it helpful to focus on principles, the foundational assumptions that make up my personal "operating system." If I have a firm base from which to make decisions, I can start to develop intentional patterns and habits that reflect those principles, requiring less and less decision-making as they become second nature.

To that end, I've distilled what I learned over the years into seven principles for an integrated life. When I use them to make decisions, I'm living a life that I can feel proud of, a life that will have a positive impact on everyone around me—including people I'll never meet—and this planet we all call home. The chapters in this part of the book describe these seven principles: see the Current, embrace "yes, *and*" to keep making progress, don't give back; just give, be brave, resist the allure of convenience, walk lightly in the world, and know your power.

CHAPTER 1

See the Current

One fish says to the other fish, "How's the water today?"
The other fish replies, "What's 'water'?"

Imagine that you're drifting down a river on an inner tube along with all your friends, riding a current and enjoying the sunshine. You've been told somewhere downstream there's a waterfall, but that danger seems, well, pretty far away. Ahead, but a manageable distance away. Nothing you have to worry about now. So you go with the flow.

Then at some point you can hear the waterfall, hear the sound of water rushing at incredible speed over the edge of a cliff. Now you can't ignore it. Now you have to decide if you're going to keep drifting along or try to fight that current. You become aware of a few people standing on the shore waving their arms, encouraging you to join them where it's safe. But the shore looks boring and lonely since all your friends and family are out on the river with you. Surely, if there really was something to worry about, all the people drifting around you would be more concerned, right?

So you might glance over to the shore people; you nod at them and smile in a friendly way but honestly can't hear much of what they are saying anyway, not with all the laughter and noise your friends are making, and it's warm and fun where you are. You suspect the shore people might be trying to warn you about that waterfall (based on their increasingly exaggerated flailing), but you don't particularly want to deal with it, because you know it could be hard to leave your friends and head to shore. It's easy being out here on the river, floating with the group.

There's a reason we call the dominant culture "main*stream*"— it's a current that requires little effort to ride and a lot of effort (maybe even some discomfort) to leave altogether and go a different direction. Even if you want to escape and try to head somewhere different, you may find that comforting, familiar current sucking you back in, keeping you heading in the same direction, toward the waterfall you can now hear, quite loudly in fact.

I've had that feeling before, I've ridden that current, and have ignored it until I couldn't ignore it anymore. If you picked up this book, I'm guessing you feel like you can't ignore it anymore either. You've started to recognize that the mainstream current isn't taking you where you want to go. So now what?

Discover the Current

As a forty-something woman with a family history of breast cancer, I have to undergo the indignity of a mammogram every year. And there's nothing that will bond you with strangers in a waiting room like the shared indignity of gowns that open in the front, and the knowledge of what it feels like to have your mammary glands summarily flattened between pressurized plastic shelves by an indifferent and efficient technician applying twenty pounds of pressure, while holding your breath and hoping you don't smell since you weren't allowed to put on deodorant that day. Trust me, this is a bonding experience, sort of like hazing, and you will smile and kvetch in a friendly way with the other women in the waiting room.

One day last year I started some small talk with a fellow traveler on the road to the plastic-plate squishing room. We talked about people we knew who had been diagnosed with breast cancer and how they were faring. We joked about how mammogram day was our favorite day of the year (which is a joke because it's actually Pap smear day). And maybe we mentioned the cost of these mammograms or the cost of treatment if it turned out you had breast cancer.

I must have said something about wishing that we didn't have to worry about the cost of health care, wishing for a system in which everyone had access to good medical care instead of a system in which some people live and some people die, in part based on their ability to afford the best care.

And my new friend said that sounded great, but she didn't support "government-run health care" like they have in other countries. She had heard that you might have to wait months for a hip replacement if you lived there, because you had to get in line for treatment *with everyone else.*

And suddenly, like Neo seeing the 0s and 1s in *The Matrix,* I saw the baseline assumptions that powered this woman's worldview. For this very lovely and kind (to me) woman, the fact that other people have to wait, or not receive care at all, if they don't have the same financial resources she has, was invisible to her. She certainly didn't want those people to suffer, but *she* didn't want to suffer either.

In short, the existing health-care system, which allows her to buy her way to the front of the line because she can afford health insurance, seems normal and correct. She was used to the United States' health system where wealth confers access and privilege. If you have the money, you can access (better) health care, faster.

Cultural norms are like that mainstream current; they are the water that flows around us that seems, well, normal. So normal that we don't even notice it, like the fish that doesn't know it's in water.

That's why the first principle of living a more integrated life is to *see the Current*—to recognize where the mainstream is taking us. Even if we aren't ready to doggy-paddle all the way to shore, recognizing the Current is a skill we need to strengthen if we want to live in greater alignment with our own values.

In addition to our system of health care, many other aspects of life that seem normal are also the Current. The idea that people (especially women) need new clothes each season is definitely treated as normal by cultural influencers. How many headlines have you seen like "The 10 Must-Have Pieces for Spring" or "The

Statement Handbags You Must Shop Now"? These days, every occasion requires new purchases, from celebrations to "self-care" rituals to moving to a new apartment. As I write this, CNN's website has an article on "The 10 Products You Need for a Stress-Free Move, According to Experts."[1] Really? Do you need ten more belongings just to move your current belongings? Unquestioning consumption is definitely the Current.

Marketing Powers the Current

Marketing has become so sophisticated that these days, it's more about psychology than the actual products. Have you ever seen an ad and had no idea what the ad was for until you get to the end and they mention their brand name or show the logo? Marketing in the twenty-first century is all about identity and psychology—showing us that buying this product will project the image we want to the people around us. Think of the last television ad you saw for perfume or aftershave. Since you can't smell it through the screen, the ad doesn't focus on what the product actually smells like. Instead, it focuses on the glamorous, admired life of the person using the product: the woman wearing the perfume soaking up sun on an island paradise or at a glamorous Hollywood party; the extremely toned man lounging on the deck of a yacht or in some desert oasis with scantily clad females admiring his six-pack abs.

I can almost understand this approach with perfumes or aftershaves (at least until they invent Smell-o-vision), but now think of some of those ads for jeans. They don't talk about how soft the jeans are or how many pockets they have (#girlsjustwantpockets) or how long they last. For women, they focus on how the life of the jean-wearer is cool, making her desired and desirable. Men are portrayed as rugged and manly, with a two-day stubble and chiseled jaw, throwing five-foot logs around like matchsticks. (Wait, is this actually a truck commercial?)

Marketing is about driving you to identify with a lifestyle and believing that this product, this thing will help you achieve that lifestyle. Have a Tesla? Everyone will think you are a cool tech bro (ha ha, just kidding, there is no such thing as a "cool" tech bro). Have a Burberry trench coat? Everyone will know you are tastefully expensive when that famous checked lining peeks out at the collar. Have Louis Vuitton sunglasses? Or handbags? Or tracksuits? Honestly, I don't even know what Louis Vuitton sells. But hey, everyone will know you are a rap icon, or aspire to be, if you sport the LV logo somewhere on your body. Marketing powers the Current.

Marketers have even caught on to using "good causes" and co-opting popular social movements to sell their products, making consumers feel that buying their products is an important way to support a cause they care about. Dove was famously praised for its "Love All Bodies" campaign. Yet its parent company, Unilever, was selling Fair & Lovely skin-lightening products marketed to women of color *at the same time*[2]—not exactly a "love the skin you're in" message. The conflicting messages used in different product lines reveals that it was never about Unilever's overarching company values—but about the psychology of different markets and how to most effectively sell into them. Good causes are good business these days.

Unfortunately, marketers are so effective at this that we have been trained to think that we can buy our way out of social problems. Here's a candle with a pink ribbon on it—buy it to fight breast cancer! Here's a (RED) shirt that will cure AIDS! These shoes solve poverty! In reality, a tiny percentage of the proceeds will go to the cause, and the companies selling them are creating more unnecessary consumption—consumption is the Current.

Audre Lorde, the famed civil rights activist, once said, "The master's tools will never dismantle the master's house";[3] in other words, we cannot solve a problem using the same tactics that created it. If a hyperconsumptive lifestyle is causing the world's environmental and social problems, we cannot buy our way out of these problems with more consumption, even if the products we consume are festooned with pink ribbons and (RED) shirts. Social cause merch is the true opioid of the masses—it lets us feel like we're doing something useful without actually doing anything useful.

Seeing the Current Changes Your Decision-Making

I don't hold myself out as the person on shore, who has broken entirely free from the mainstream, trying to warn the masses of the impending doom. I suspect I'm the goofball who has the inner tube holding me up by my armpits, legs in the water, arms akimbo, and using my hands to try to doggy-paddle toward shore, putting about three feet of distance between me and the group but still moving essentially in alignment with the mainstream—albeit slowly making progress.

Whatever progress I have made often stems from moments of discomfort:

- *I support living wages.* So when I would shop at the mall and pop in to "just check out the clearance rack" at the fast fashion place, I felt a little ill walking out with a bag of cute sweaters that I know were not produced by people making a fair wage. In 2012, I started shopping at consignment stores and online resale sites (and, okay, some still at the mall).

- *I am a feminist.* When I read a magazine with the headline "How to Lose 20 pounds in 2 Weeks" next to the other headline "How to Make the Best Chocolate Cake Your Family Will Love!" I felt a little ill about the conflicting messages about women's worth that I'm consuming. (FYI, it's not coffee; it's mayonnaise. Mayonnaise is the secret ingredient to great chocolate cake. Fight me.) In 2013, I stopped reading "women's magazines" altogether.

- *I value the environment.* For years I would go to the grocery store and buy organic produce in individual plastic bags and then the cashier put those plastic bags into larger plastic bags and double bagged the whole thing. I always felt a little ill walking out with forty or fifty plastic bags in my cart. In 2020 I finally got a firm habit of bringing my own bags, including reusable mesh produce bags.

- *I value a fair playing field and economic justice.* So when I read about my large national bank with thousands of convenient ATMs and the role they played in triggering the Great Recession of 2008, I felt a little ill using the slick, convenient app on my phone to deposit a check. In 2021, I finally switched my accounts to a local credit union instead.

Situations like these have come up in my life over and over. And I definitely have times where I have chosen to ignore them. But what often happens is that over time the discomfort gets stronger and the roar of the waterfall harder to ignore. Eventually, I turn around and face the conflict between my deepest values and my everyday actions. And then I decide what to do about it.

If I decide to do something different, it's often a little painful at first. Switching to a local credit union (from that big national bank) has been a complete pain in my ass—but after that painful period, the banking service is essentially the same as it used to be, only now I feel more at peace. I feel more in alignment with my values and less hypocritical. Buying reusable produce bags felt a little extreme and it was hard to remember to use them consistently in the beginning, but now it's second nature to grab my reusable bags (with the produce bags inside) when I head out the door on Sunday morning to grocery shop.

Embrace Discomfort as a Signal to Change

I'm guessing you, like me, have had moments when you realize the mainstream culture is taking you in a direction you don't want to go. You may have felt the Current without really naming it. Like my moments of discomfort with fast fashion, plastic bags, or trashy magazines, there are things that cause you some amount of discomfort, fear, or guilt. (Or maybe you do recognize it and call it a "guilty pleasure.")

But what I've learned is that if there is something weighing on me, the cognitive dissonance of letting it fester is far more painful than the quick sting of pulling the bandage off in a single yank.

Now, if I feel pulled by the Current in a direction I don't want to go, instead of turning away, I try to turn toward it. First, to name it. Honestly, this step might take a few months because giving a name, a label, to the tug of the Current, even in the privacy of your own mind, makes it real. And that can be scary because it signals that you know something needs to change, and change is scary. So give yourself some grace, but also be real about naming things for what they are.

When you've named the thing that needs to change, start to evaluate your possible paths forward: *What are the alternatives? What might I do differently, big or small? Is there some way to test a new approach without going all in?*

Discomfort is a wonderful guide to identify the areas where you aren't living in alignment with your own values. Use it to identify one or two areas you want to address in your own life.

CHAPTER 2

Embrace "Yes, *and*" to Keep Making Progress

You don't have to be great to start, but you have to start to be great.

—ATTRIBUTED TO ZIG ZIGLAR

When it comes to taking action to improve shared prosperity, many of us fall into the trap of criticizing people for not doing enough. I think that's a narrow way to view the world and have adopted a "yes, *and*" mentality from improv comedy.

"Yes, *and*" is one of the first techniques they teach you if you are crazy enough to take an improv class. At least, that's the impression I got from Tina Fey when reading her book *Bossypants*:

The first rule of improvisation is AGREE. Always agree and SAY YES. When you're improvising, this means you are required to agree with whatever your partner has created. So if we're improvising and I say, "Freeze, I have a gun," and you say, "That's not a gun. It's your finger. You're pointing your finger at me," our improvised scene has ground to a halt. But if I say, "Freeze, I have a gun!" and you say, "The gun I gave you for Christmas! You bastard!" then we have started a scene because we have AGREED that my finger is in fact a Christmas gun . . .

The second rule of improvisation is not only to say yes, but YES, AND. You are supposed to agree and then add something of your own. If I start a scene with "I can't believe it's so hot in here," and you just say, "Yeah . . ." we're kind of at a standstill. But if I say, "I can't believe it's so hot in here," and you say, "What did you expect? We're in hell." . . . now we're getting somewhere. To me YES, AND means don't be afraid to contribute. It's your responsibility to contribute.[1]

I'm a huge fan of living this way. It's not this *or* that, but we need this *and* that to get where we're trying to go. We actually need "all of the above" when it comes to solutions that lead to greater shared prosperity. So I'm not going to fault you or anyone for taking small, positive steps.

In May of 2021, a bunch of food pantries in the Denver area banded together as the pandemic continued into its second year, describing how demand had increased by 300 percent with no signs of slowing. The CEO of one of those pantries, Metro Caring's Teva Sienicki, gave an incredibly brave interview that touched on the difference between initial steps and ongoing efforts to change: "[Corporations] ask, 'can we come and volunteer?' and I say, 'sure.' . . . But the biggest thing you can do [to shorten lines at food pantries] is to think about . . . how much . . . the lowest person on your team [is] earning."[2] In this statement, Sienicki has said "yes" to the idea of volunteering and donating but then followed up with an "and" about other changes that organizations could make.

Start Small, but Just Start

Today, many socially conscious actions have been labeled what is disparagingly called "slacktivism," in which we do something minimal so we can feel like we're doing something without really doing anything:

> Slacktivism is a way to voice your opinion about a certain cause without taking to the streets or risking your neck. It's the viral hashtag you're retweeting. The pink ribbon on your shirt. The rainbow-colored frame on your Facebook picture. The "Save The Turtles" petition you signed last week.[3]

I've definitely been a slacktivist before: I changed my Facebook avatar to a red square with a pink equal sign for a few weeks in 2013 to show that I supported gay marriage. Did it matter? Was it a dumb, meaningless idea and quickly forgotten? Maybe. I remembered the effort, but I had to go back and look to see why we all used that avatar specifically. (It was a play on the Human Rights Campaign logo, and the effort coincided with the Supreme Court consideration of a gay marriage case.[4]) But I did it because I know some of my extended family and friends do *not* support gay marriage. Others are gay, and I wanted to let them all know that I support them publicly, where other people can see that support. And I wanted the people who don't support gay marriage to know that lots of people, including me, disagreed with them.

Changing your Facebook avatar, of course, doesn't change the real world. It took another action by the Supreme Court two years later to strike down bans on gay marriage in *Obergefell v. Hodges*, effectively legalizing it in all fifty states. And I would not argue that the red and pink Facebook avatars influenced the Supreme Court. But I don't think it hurt to bring visibility and awareness to these high-profile moments and high-stakes cases. Which is why I am not going to dunk on slacktivism—as long as it doesn't stop there. Small actions can be an important on-ramp for those just getting up to speed on an issue. It gives them a way to take that first step in public, a step that might feel uncomfortable or difficult.

When a child is learning to walk and falls on her butt or bumps her head on the coffee table, do we mock and belittle that child for trying? Of course we don't. We encourage her to give it another try, take a few more steps, until walking becomes second nature. Yet somehow, it's become savvy to mock and belittle well-intentioned folks who take small steps if they don't run a marathon in their first effort. Instead of mocking them (which can also lead them to give up, since they feel damned if they do, damned if they don't), let's adopt the "yes, *and*" approach to encourage them to take the next step, and the one after that, and the one after that. Soon they'll be walking alongside us, or at least doggy-paddling alongside us and away from the Current.

No Free Passes, However

Though I'm against being too critical of people who are at least trying to do the right things, I'm not suggesting you pat someone on the back and tell them, "Your job here is done" after small improvements. A good deed in one neighborhood doesn't forgive a bad deed in another; we can't buy forgiveness for continued misbehavior with good behavior elsewhere. At least, not these days.

"Indulgences" are an old concept from the Roman Catholic Church. Literally you could buy forgiveness for your sins (and reduce your time in the Bad Place) by making contributions to the church. To be technical about it, the contributions were viewed as a good deed, and that good deed would offset the bad deeds you committed (a.k.a. sins). As you can imagine, not everyone could afford to buy indulgences from the church. Wealthy parishioners could use indulgences to be cleansed before God even when they had committed terrible sins (the bigger the sin, the bigger the required offsetting donation, of course). Poor, working people couldn't afford it. Which meant they faced much harder roads to redemption. It was great fundraising for the church, though, which was apparently glad to take your money in exchange for essentially looking the other way and not asking you to stop the behavior or make things right by, you know, cleaning up the harm you caused.

Sometimes in today's world it feels like we are being told to continue the practice of granting Indulgences. If a person or company donates to charity, we should praise them for their contribution. Great, I'm down with that. But if someone tries to point out that the same person or their company is polluting that river or underpaying their workers, we are pointed back to the good deeds done elsewhere. Fundamentally, this is a diversion tactic. Philanthropy isn't the same thing as restorative justice; if your actions cause harm, you have to stop the actions and repair any harm you may have caused, not just plant flowers in another neighborhood and call it good.

That's why the principle isn't just "yes!" but "yes, *and*." Because we need to celebrate small steps while still seeking accountability for larger improvements.

The Power of Habit Stacking

In his short, powerful book *Atomic Habits: An Easy and Proven Way to Build Good Habits and Break Bad Ones*, James Clear shares proven techniques to change our behavior when we want to adopt new habits. The whole book is worth reading, but I'd especially point you to the concept of habit stacking—attaching a new habit to an existing one. Can you think of some area of your life where you've taken a small step in line with your values? Can you cue off that positive habit—*embrace "yes, and"*—to find the next right principle you could adopt?

Maybe you bought a few reusable bags with good intentions but always seem to leave them at home. Can you gather them up and place them in your car now, so they'll be there when you head to the store? If you're a pro with your reusable grocery bags but are still grabbing those thin plastic produce bags to hold your peppers and tomatoes, maybe add some mesh produce bags to your routine?

Maybe you and your partner always eat out on Friday nights. Could you choose a new local joint to support each week? Could you leave a positive review on social media to help others find them?

Maybe you always pick your kid up from school and love to talk about their day. Could you start making that a walk instead of a drive each day, or just a few days a week when you don't have errands or activities to attend?

Maybe you love to make bread, or paper crafts, or garden. Could you turn that passion into your go-to gift when special occasions arrive instead of buying something from a store? (If you come to my place, please bring me a little planting that I can't easily kill! Or an herb from your garden would be amazing!)

Take a minute now and think of something you are already doing that you feel good about. How can you embrace a "yes, *and*" mentality and extend its impact a little further by doing the next right thing?

CHAPTER 3

Don't Give Back; Just *Give*

We make a living by what we get,
but we make a life by what we give.
—ATTRIBUTED TO WINSTON CHURCHILL

In early 2021, I saw a tweet from a highly regarded venture capitalist, saying, "I'm focused on capitalism for now—but planning to shift to philanthropy at sixty-five [in fifteen years]." He's not alone in that mentality, but I think it's misguided. I haven't analyzed his portfolio, but I'm pretty confident that some of the wealth he's building through today's investments is also directly causing problems he'll claim to be passionate about solving when he's sixty-five.

This mentality of separating money-making from giving back to society is nothing new. When I was building my tech startup in

2012 and 2013, many advisors and investors told me, "Focus on making money; when you're profitable you can worry about doing good." This is the wisdom of the Current. In fact, that's how we are encouraged to think by very smart people: get yours first, and then you can give (some) back (if you want).

Inherent in the logic and word choice of "giving *back*" is the idea that you first took something. But what did you take? Did you take profits? Fine. Did you take advantage of a regulatory loophole or lax environmental regulation? That's legal but not awesome. Did you take the labor of people who were not adequately compensated? Hmmm . . .

It's a common narrative in American life that businesses make money, and charities try to address problems. But in reality, we've allowed some businesses to make money by *causing* massive problems (think smokestacks and contaminated water, deforestation, loss of green spaces, lack of living wages, gentrification, racially segregated neighborhoods from banks redlining and landlords discriminating). These aren't problems that came from nowhere—they came from business models that turned natural assets, underpaid labor, and racial segregation into shareholder profits. In short, the formula for wealth, success, and admiration is extract, extract, extract as much as you can, and then when you have enough, give a little back.

I'm not suggesting that all businesses are bad or all businesspeople are unethical. Not at all. But I'm saying that the mentality of "take first and then give back" is the antithesis of an integrated life. Thinking you'll focus on environmental causes when you're retired from the business of wealth creation? Why not start now, and apply some of your values to screen your investment choices? I would much rather us celebrate those who don't extract but who build in shared prosperity from the beginning.

We need to reject the mentality that "I'll get mine first, and then I'll give back" if we're going to live an integrated life. Instead, we need to *just give*. *Just give* means to be fair and even generous in our everyday transactions, not trying to maximize benefit for ourselves alone.

Doing Good While Doing Well

Dan Price is an entrepreneur who decided in 2015 to take a radically different approach to compensation at his company, Gravity Payments. After one employee making $35,000 a year accused him of being happy to get away with paying him too little so as to increase his own earnings, Dan took a hard look in the mirror. He decided he wasn't living in accordance with his values, and in an unusually brave move, he made a drastic break from the status quo: over the next few years, he raised the salary of every employee to a minimum of $70,000 and cut his own salary from over a million dollars to $70,000 to help pay for the increases.[1]

Some predicted that the company would fail and even went so far as to say, "I hope this company is a case study in MBA programs on how socialism does not work, because it's going to fail."[2] But Gravity Payments found that productivity—and profits—increased enough to offset the salary increases over the next few years. In fact, revenue tripled. More recently, Dan has shared that more of his employees have bought houses, more have started families, and more have gotten healthier and paid down debt after increasing their income.[3]

In a speech at the Vision 2020 conference, Dan said, "If I could, in my career, be a part of a movement where business is about solving the problems of humanity, business is about service, about purpose . . . and economics are [only] a means to an end, I think that would be a good enough thing, fun enough thing to accomplish that I'd be willing to give up everything else in my career for that one thing."[4]

One of my favorite lines from Dan's Twitter feed puts his philosophy into perspective. He says, "Stop asking if the price of goods will go up if the minimum wage grows, and start asking why you're subsidizing businesses to pay poverty wages."[5] The American people are subsidizing companies that pay poverty wages through government programs that provide food and housing support to their workforce, even those who work full time. We've been told to believe "that's just good business," as if there is no other way for companies to reasonably act than to try to extract the maximum for the executives and shareholders at the expense of the workforce, the community, and the environment.

Dan ignited a firestorm of backlash because he is exposing the lopsided way financial benefit is distributed in much of our economy. He is making a different choice, which is to forgo the traditional model of maximizing your personal income first and *then* giving back. And his choice—extreme in the other direction—makes it obvious that extreme compensation *is* a choice. He's pointing out the water we swim in and bucking the Current. He isn't waiting to give back; he's decided to *just give*.

The Push for Profit

A frustrating pattern among shareholders and corporate boards over the years has been to push every button for the company's short-term benefit—push workers so hard to fill orders they have to pee in bottles rather than take breaks.[6] Push conveyor belt speeds so high that workplace accidents are common.[7] Push tasks like security checkpoints and logging hours on to personal time so the company doesn't compensate workers to complete required tasks. Push junior associates to log so many billable hours that they don't have time for rest, for recharging, for hobbies. Push expectations for employees to be responsive into all hours of the day and night. Push productivity up and costs down.

But then when the benefits of that pushing come to fruition in the form of higher margins, greater profitability, and ultimately a higher stock price or company valuation, corporations don't always share those benefits with the full set of workers who made it possible. Many reserve raises, bonuses, stock incentives, and other financial rewards for the executives and the shareholders. According to the Economic Policy Institute, between 1973 and 2014, productivity grew by 72.2 percent, yet median worker compensation grew by only 8.7 percent, while CEO pay has risen by more than 800 percent:

> Since 2000, more than 80 percent of the divergence
> between a typical worker's pay growth and overall
> net productivity growth [was] driven by inequal-
> ity . . . (a falling share of income going to workers
> relative to capital owners). [In] 1973–2014, rising

inequality explains over two-thirds of the produc-
tivity-pay divergence.[8]

In other words, workers continue to be more and more productive, creating more benefit for the companies that employ them.
And yet they aren't sharing proportionately in the prosperity—the
executives are keeping that additional wealth for themselves and
their shareholders—and then they designate a small portion of
proceeds to "give back" to the community, in the form of a grant
to a nonprofit organization ("donation with each purchase!"), or
maybe a gift of product or exposure to their audience, or some
volunteer time from employees or executives.

But what if more corporations scaled back or gave up their
grantmaking or product donations, and instead gave everyone
who works for them a raise, a bonus, and/or some stock options?
I'd much rather support *that* company with my consumer dollars.
The argument against raising wages always asserts that the problem
with doing so is that higher labor costs will result in price increases
for consumers—and those price increases will necessarily result in
lost business and layoffs because consumers will refuse to pay more
for products and services. I am not an economist or a policy maker,
but I am a consumer. And so I can prove that last assumption to
be false in my everyday choices by willingly spending more with
companies that distribute the wealth, that *just give*.

I don't want this book or the integrated life to be about spending money that you don't have or about buying stuff that you don't
need. But sometimes we do have a little discretionary money, and

we can decide how to spend it. I would never advocate for spending $50 on one T-shirt if you don't need a new T-shirt, or even if you do need a new T-shirt but that $50 price tag is just paying for a designer logo. But if the T-shirt costs $50 because it's made with organic, fast-growing bamboo and sewn by people making a living wage in healthy working conditions, that's a form of giving. The company making the shirt is giving those people dignity, fair wages, and hope for their future. They are giving the environment a sustainable solution for clothing. And you are giving your money (and giving up the opportunity to buy several cheaper T-shirts made in a fast fashion factory) by reinforcing their choices and voting with your pocketbook.

One organization that has adopted this mantra (actually, "Give First") is Techstars, a global startup accelerator that has invested in thousands of tech companies, many of which have grown into successful market leaders.[9] They would tell you their secret is their network of people willing to give first. Techstars cofounders Brad Feld and David Cohen encourage everyone to support their portfolio companies however they can—with introductions, with mentorship, with customer referrals, with a listening ear—without asking for anything in return. And the power of being part of such a network means that someday, when you do need help, you will be part of this incredible community of people. And one of them, someone you've never met, never helped, never knew, might be the perfect person to help you out. Find the *Give First* podcast on your favorite platform to hear more from the Techstars network.

Where Can *You* Just Give?

Everyone, whether you are a business owner, a manager, a frontline employee, or not an employee at all, can still adopt a *just give* mentality in your life.

- Help a neighbor, without expectation of them returning the favor.

- Mentor a young person, without thinking of how they might advance your career.

- Donate to a cause that doesn't benefit you personally.

- Hand out compliments flagrantly.

- Offer to carpool with someone at your workplace or your kid's after-school activity just because you see they could use some help.

The next time you need to buy something for yourself, your family, your household, or others, think about how you can use it as an opportunity to give, instead of being solely focused on getting a good deal for yourself.

And, most importantly, don't wait for some magic status that will mean you have made it professionally, personally, or financially *before* you start thinking about how you can help others. Start today, and *just give*.

CHAPTER 4

Be Brave

It is difficult to get a man to understand something,
when his salary depends upon his not understanding it.

—UPTON SINCLAIR, *I, CANDIDATE FOR GOVERNOR*

S ome years ago, even though I worked in the philanthropic
sector, I started feeling called to live in greater alignment with
my values. At the time I was making a good salary. I was also the
primary breadwinner for my family of five, including three kids
and an amazing supportive spouse. It was difficult under these circumstances to question my own motives and my own fidelity to
my values. To leave a financially secure situation not because of ill
will or a bad boss, but simply because I felt called was incredibly
scary. Could I find opportunities more in line with my values but

still maintain the same level of salary and benefits? Eventually, I realized that was the wrong question.

You see, while I was scrolling through job sites, I would dismiss interesting and values-aligned opportunities to do good work, thinking "that probably doesn't pay very well." And then I realized, quite painfully, that I was doing the same thing as those "vulture capitalists" I had been so disdainful of—I was putting my own financial benefit above the other principles I said I believed in, like social justice and an opportunity to live into my purpose and values. It was a bit of a gut punch to realize that I had bought into the importance of prioritizing my personal financial success at some deep, unconscious level.

I wrestled with the weight of my responsibilities to my family compared to my desire for using my full self in my work. And ultimately, I adopted the mantra "be brave." *Be brave* means to have faith that taking steps toward an integrated life will lead to a fulfilled and successful life, though it might not be measured in outsized material success but rather in the friendship and love of good people and good times, and a contented soul.

Looking back, I've been through many circumstances where I had to *be brave*. Most dramatically, in 2011 I quit my six-figure job to start my own socially responsible company along with my sister and my mother, two of the smartest financial and operational minds I know.

We went through some lean times, where our monthly budget for entertainment was only enough for a Redbox movie with two Little Caesar's pizzas, about $15 in total. My family didn't have health insurance for six months, and I remember my heart would leap into my throat every time my six-year-old son would come pounding down the stairs. *Please don't break a leg*, I thought, *because we really can't afford it*. We cashed out the small 401(k) I had managed to save at a previous job. We accrued credit card debt, making just the minimum payment so we didn't have to leave the neighborhood where we rented a house, where our kids went to school, and where our friends and family lived. I missed a payment on my Kohl's charge because I didn't have cash in the bank.

But I tried to *be brave* because I believed deeply in the mission of our company, an online resale site for gently used baby, kids, and maternity clothes. And I was proud to be doing something tangible to be part of the solution, to build an alternative to needless consumption, helping a wasteful industry be a little less wasteful.

A couple years into my startup journey, I was asked to be a guest speaker for a class at Northwestern University focused on entrepreneurship. I remember telling those students how I found the courage to take the leap from salaried employee to entrepreneur. "I am paying myself about $30,000 a year now as CEO, and that's a raise from the $18,000 I was taking before we raised investor capital. But besides building the value of our startup, and my own equity along with it, I am learning invaluable skills and building relationships in an industry that is my future—the social change industry. And if the company goes bust, I will still take those skills and those relationships with me, making me a far more valuable employee than I was before I had this experience."

The ending of that story has good news and bad news: The bad news is that we ended up selling the company to a competitor who gladly took our inventory and our customer list but dismantled the brand in about six weeks. And it wasn't the kind of sale that made our team millionaires. The good news is that we undeniably helped make the concept of clothing resale mainstream and helped thousands of parents save money and avoid waste, even if we didn't become the market leader. And sure enough, when I went back to the job market, my next salaried position was more than three times what I had made before.

Being brave and standing in my purpose eventually paid off financially, but it had paid off in terms of my own sense of self much faster than that. I had developed confidence in my own purpose and in the power of living an integrated life—and that confidence helped me *be brave* the next time, and the time after that.

Facing Reality

In the quest to *be brave*, I still sometimes find myself wrestling with the difference between my values and beliefs and having the courage to change my beliefs when they are challenged by new facts. The difference between values and beliefs is illuminated by the field of psychology, which teaches:

- Values are the underlying ideals that drive you, things like fairness, justice, freedom, equality, loyalty, and the importance of family.

- Beliefs are stories that you believe to be true, assumptions about the world and how it works. Is the criminal justice system fundamentally fair? Does everyone have a fair chance at the American Dream? Do people generally get what they deserve?

Most Americans have similar values. (That's why I don't spend a lot of time talking about values in this book.) It's our beliefs that contradict each other and cause us to act in very different ways. Two people who say they value fairness might be on opposite ends of the debate about affirmative action in higher education admissions: One believes that a fair system evaluates each candidate as an individual and they are admitted or not based on their personal characteristics and accomplishments. The other believes that the system has been unfair for decades, since those evaluations are based on characteristics and accomplishments most easily attained by wealthy white families because of generations of unequal treatment in education, business, lending, home ownership, and other factors. Same value (fairness), different beliefs about how the world works and therefore how to achieve the end goal.

Our beliefs are like the Current to our lives—they pull us in one direction, and they are most definitely hard to change. When you start to encounter information that contradicts your beliefs, you have two choices: reexamine your beliefs, or find another explanation for the conflicting information. Spoiler alert: most people select the latter. They question and refuse to accept even highly credible information if it conflicts with their beliefs.

And this is a technique we use too often to lead a life that isn't integrated, that isn't truly in line with the values we say we hold; we simply reject the information that tells us that our action isn't in line with our values. That is not being brave.

The Courage to Challenge a Belief

Here's an example of a conflict between values and beliefs that created a lot of cognitive dissonance for me:

- *Value:* My life choices shouldn't harm anyone else—not people or the planet we share.

- *Belief:* Eating meat is a normal and acceptable part of the American diet, and there's nothing wrong with it.

What happens to that belief when you learn stats about the impact of meat production—on the animals who are subjected to abject cruelty and torture, on the environment in terms of soil, air, and water, but also on our own health when we consume it, and on the workers' physical and mental health in producing it for us?[1]

Frankly, even as a lifelong meat eater, the reality of meat production makes me uncomfortable. But for many years I mostly avoided thinking about it or finding information about it. I lived with that minor discomfort since it didn't intrude on my life. It was easy enough *not* to click on the headline "10 Things You Should Know about Industrial Farming." Maybe I *should* know, but I don't really *want* to know. *Keep scrolling.*

Then, one day when my daughter was a freshman in high school, she came home pronouncing herself a vehement new vegetarian. Turns out that a guest lecturer in a health class had come in to talk about "the ethics of food production" and showed them a video of industrial farming practices. "Mom, it was so disturbing I almost passed out," she said, "and I decided on the spot that I am going to be a vegetarian." I applaud her for allowing her belief (meat eating is normal and fine) to be challenged in the face of new information (industrial animal production is not humane) that didn't align with her deeper value (animals deserve to be treated with dignity). She had the courage to challenge an accepted belief and change her behavior because of it.

Since that time, our family has not entirely cut out meat, but we've all cut it back considerably. We now have meat two to three times per week, and then it's usually more like a complementary flavor added in for the meat eaters at the end, not the main course in a big slab on the plate.

It's no fun to look at yourself in the mirror and acknowledge you've been engaging in a harmful practice, whether that's staying in a soul-sucking but well-paying job, buying more jeans or shoes than one person could ever need, or consuming the products and services of cruel and unjust industries. Finding out disturbing information about someone or something we have admired or endorsed—an athlete, an entertainer, a civic leader, an educational or religious institution—is incredibly painful. Often, our first instinct is to explain it away. It requires bravery to admit our complicity in these systems and vow to do better.

Challenging Yourself

Where are the areas of your life that you feel cognitive dissonance—where one of your values and a belief or action are in conflict? Those areas are a great guide to figure out where we need to turn our attention. *Be brave*, and name that conflict within yourself for what it is.

CHAPTER 5

Resist the Allure
of Convenience

At one point in her journey away from being a meat eater, my daughter Audrey considered going all the way to veganism, because she understood the treatment of cows and chickens to get eggs and dairy products for human consumption was not much better than industrial meat production. And—I'm not gonna lie—I resisted. I didn't want to give up eggs—they're my breakfast almost every day, and we bake a lot, and it would just feel like one less source of protein in an increasingly protein-scarce vegetarian diet. But I wanted to respect her feelings about the treatment of the cows and the chickens.

We already got our milk from Longmont Dairy, a local operation in Colorado that delivers its own milk to customers' doorsteps in glass bottles that are returned and reused up to twenty times.[1] I feel pretty good about that choice, and so did Audrey.

So I did some research on egg producers in our area and found a local co-op that sells eggs from a few local farmers who have small flocks and harvest eggs from happy chickens with plenty of grass and sunshine and room to run. We now get our eggs each week from Farmer Gavin, a teenager working with his family to treat the chickens ethically. The chickens live in mobile coops with regular access to fresh grass and long runs featuring slides and swings.

> We feed them wheat, milo and corn [raised] on our farm. Our uncle raises the alfalfa for us and we always keep a bale available to them which they LOVE! We have a friend that runs a saw mill and they provide us with fragrant shavings for our chickens.[2]

Thank God for the Farmer Gavins in this world. I now pay $5.60 per dozen, instead of $3.00 or so for conventional eggs at the grocery store, but my family feels a lot better knowing the chickens that produced our breakfast are leading good little chicken lives.

Once we became members of the co-op, we found many other items we could get from there as well: most of the meat we do eat comes from their small-scale local producers, we also get seasonal produce such as potatoes and onions, basil and microgreens, and fantastic Colorado honey. So one values-driven change that took some work to get in place has become a regular and easy feature of our eating habits.

And I learned something else from the experience—that sometimes living an integrated life is about placing the rest of your values ahead of your own convenience.

Is an Integrated Life Inconvenient?

I was describing my ethical egg hunt to a friend one day, and her reaction was a dismissive "that sounds like a lot of running around." And I had two thoughts. The first was that I should clarify this is mostly an online hunt rather than a bunch of trips to chicken farms or physical groceries. So please allow me to clarify that this was a virtual egg hunt and not a physical one.

But the second reaction was that this friend has internalized the message that our personal convenience is the most important benefit a product or service can provide to us. And I thought, *Yeah, that's the Current at its core.* That's the default setting for our decisions if we don't take a moment to be intentional about placing other values ahead of our own convenience.

The current consumer backlash over Amazon was preceded by the fact that consumers have been choosing Amazon for more and more of our household purchases because it's incredibly convenient to do so. They carry such a huge range of products, some of which are hard to find elsewhere (but many of which are not) and deliver them straight to our door in a few days, and without adding noticeably to the cost of the item. What's not to like?

Except somewhere along the way, to offer more products, and to deliver them faster and faster into our grubby little hands, Amazon started making choices about what they needed from their employees to deliver the convenient experience we demanded (although we certainly didn't demand it until Amazon created it and we got used to it). And Amazon's choices seriously degraded the quality of jobs that it offers, while simultaneously putting their competitors out of business. So consumers now have fewer choices for retailers, and warehouse workers have fewer options for quality employment, and they are at greater risk of injury and anxiety while also being forced into indignity because they will be penalized for not making good time if they stop for a much-needed break.[3]

When I signed up for Prime all those years ago, that's not what I signed up for, at least not knowingly and intentionally. It sort of happened while we were enjoying our two-day delivery.

I am at a point where I want to rethink that decision, now that I know what consequences it brings (in the scorekeeping of the Good Place, I am pretty sure being an Amazon customer would keep anyone out of the Good Place!).

And so I offer you this as a grounding principle for living an integrated life that is aligned with your values: sometimes it will be inconvenient. If you are brave enough to walk away from people, circumstances, and institutions that aren't in line with the value of shared prosperity, a little extra effort, or a little extra patience, or a little extra money may be required. If you don't have the extra money, I will never begrudge you shopping at whatever discount store you need to make ends meet. If you are a caretaker with more demands than you have time, I will never begrudge you doing what you need to in order to get everything done. But if you can spare a little extra time, extra thought, or extra money, you'll be rewarded with a little more alignment.

Rather than focus on the inconvenience, however, I've started thinking of the extra effort as a "convenience tax." Because it is undeniably an extra burden, sometimes an extra expense, but for me it's one that I can choose to pay because I can afford it. I can afford to shop at the local stationery store for expensive but recyclable wrapping paper instead of cheaper stuff from the big box store that is not recyclable and can only go to the landfill. I can afford the time to call around to the local sporting goods store to see if they carry the right size bat for my daughter before automatically heading to the national chain with three floors of inventory, which is bound to have the correct size in stock. I can afford to go out of my way to buy sports headbands from a local mom selling her homemade version instead of getting mass-produced versions at the mall. Sometimes the convenience tax is time, sometimes it's money, sometimes it's simply inconvenience. But if you can afford it, it's a great investment in your community and your own peace of mind.

Starting Point: Buy Local

Look, I'm not a monk. I'm not planning to live off the grid or grow all my own food and make my own clothes. I do own stuff, including functionally useless but decorative stuff. So that means I do have to buy stuff—the food and personal care items I consume but also the stuff that stays year after year like couches, chairs, desks, artwork, linens, and clothes. When we need something new and borrowing or getting it gently used isn't a good option, *where* we get it matters. That's why a first step is to focus on buying from local businesses.

According to the Civic Economics Survey of Independent Businesses, when you shop at a national chain retailer, only 13.6 percent of that revenue stays in the local community. But when you shop at a local retailer, that number rises to 47.7 percent, including employee wages, utilities and taxes, charitable donations, and the ripple effects on other small business owners in your area—such as their accountant, tax provider, inventory suppliers, and more.[4] When you see a national chain store, picture a giant vacuum hovering over the top of the building and literally sucking $86 of every $100 spent—it travels up, up, and away from your community, away from your neighbors, away from your schools and roads and public safety and more.

Real wealth will almost never come from a salary; for most people the way to build wealth is through ownership, also called equity. Equity in a house and equity in a business are two important ways to build wealth. When you support a small business, you are building the wealth of your neighbors and your neighborhood.

The opportunity for people to build a business and grow it successfully is not something I take for granted as a former business owner myself. It requires support from community members (like you!) who are willing to perhaps pay a small inconvenience tax compared to the scaled efficiency of a global business. Maybe you have to select from a more limited inventory, because they only have two kinds of peanut butter—crunchy or creamy (creamy, duh). Maybe they have to order the item you want, and you'll have to wait a week to get it. Maybe it costs 10 percent more. Maybe they aren't open on Mondays and holidays. For me, the value of supporting my neighbors is worth the tax of that small inconvenience.

So the next time you get donuts for a Sunday morning, get them from a local bakery not the chain grocery store. The next time you give flowers, find a local florist and call them directly to order instead of giving a cut to the national consolidator. The next time you want a quick bite, try that quirky little deli you've been driving past for years, instead of the same old chains. More of your money will stay in your community and grow wealth for your neighbors, instead of just wages.

CHAPTER 6

Walk Lightly in the World

As a general concept, "footprint" has been used to describe the amount of space something takes up on whatever surface it sits on. Buildings have a physical footprint—the amount of square feet they take up and in what configuration. A piece of furniture has a footprint in your living room. A computer setup or a printer has a footprint on top of your desk.

In the 1990s, researchers started applying the term to human consumption, coining the term "ecological footprint" to describe the impact of humans on the landscape of the natural world.[1] Our footprint comprises the resources we consume in going about our daily lives, including fossil fuels, clean water, living creatures, raw materials, and other natural resources. Spoiler alert: we are using up more resources each year than the earth can regenerate in that same period of time.[2]

Americans are not the same as the rest of the planet in this regard. In a 2012 article, Sierra Club's Dave Tilton was quoted as saying, "A child born in the United States will create thirteen times as much ecological damage over the course of his or her lifetime than a child born in Brazil," adding that the average American will drain as many resources as thirty-five natives of India and consume fifty-three times more goods and services than someone from China.[3]

The same article points out that Americans represent 5 percent of the world's population but produce 50 percent of the world's solid waste. Which means we use all these resources to produce stuff, and then it breaks, or wears out, or "goes out of fashion," and we toss it in a landfill. Oy.

It feels selfish when I realize how much energy, how much raw material, and how much labor goes into creating things for me to buy, just to have them pass through my life and on to a landfill within a few days or months.[4] Especially because one of my underlying values is that I hate being a consumer and I hate the concept of disposability. I hate consuming things. Consuming, to be literal, is to use up a resource. We consume food; we can't help it. But as Americans we are also encouraged to consume resources with almost pathological disregard for where that resource came from and whether there is more of it and what its production does to the community it is extracted from, the people who produce it, and to the various stops along the supply chain. While consumption is what drives our economy (and so many people argue that jobs and economic activity are the ultimate "good" that comes from consumption), unbridled consumption of resources obviously has a limit—we are literally consuming our planet. And when we use it up, as they say, "there is no Planet B."

If you listen to any business news program (as I have done for two decades on the way to and from work), you will hear the current state of the Dow Jones Industrial Average every half an hour, told with up-to-the-minute accuracy and urgency, including an explanation for why the stock prices of these thirty companies have moved a bit on any given day. This is reported constantly because we are told the Dow represents the health of our economy, so we need to pay close attention and make sure it's always growing. And we are also told that the prices move higher when the world buys more stuff. So more stuff = healthy, growing economy = good.

But good for *whom*? Good for our planet? That's a clear "no"; we already consume more than our planet can replenish each year, so growing our consumption only makes the problem worse. Good for our pocketbooks? Also a "no," since Americans have more credit card debt per household than any other country,[5] totaling $992 billion in 2021.[6] Good for the workers who produce those goods? Maybe—if their working conditions provide a healthy, dignified life and if there aren't jobs for them in other industries. Good for the people who own shares of those stocks? Definitely.

The Current tells you to consume more resources, including fuel, consumer goods, and disposable products of all kinds because doing so will make you happy; it's the American Dream! It's not American-made goods but rather our luxurious lifestyle—represented by sprawling mansions, heated pools, private jets, and a continual parade of new clothing, shoes, and tech toys—that is America's biggest export to the world. And perhaps our most destructive. The article cited above about the disproportionate size of the American footprint came out nine years ago. And, yes, the gap has shrunk since then but not because Americans consume less (though we do, down 20 percent since 2005); it's because other countries are gaining wealth and adopting American consumer habits, causing them to catch up.[7] We are projecting an aspirational image of unbridled consumption across the globe via television, movies, and other media—and it's time to course correct before, heaven help us, everyone aspires to live like James Bond, the Kardashians, or the Real Housewives of Wherever.

How Much Stuff Do You Have?

In 2002, I was twenty-six and recently married. My husband and I were moving out of our first house, a split Victorian in Philadelphia's Germantown neighborhood. We had hired movers for the first time and felt pretty grown up for not using a U-Haul and a few friends to load us up for the trip back to Ohio. We were sitting on the porch during a lunch break, having bought cheeseburgers for the movers and ourselves. The movers were students, mostly from other countries, and they were still pretty new to America. As we chatted, one of them commented on how much stuff we had—not nearly enough to fill their big truck but enough to need to hire them! He said something like, "You know you don't need all this stuff. What is it for? How much are you paying to move and store it?" He shook his head incredulously.

His comment hit home because we were in fact moving most of the items into storage. We were temporarily moving back in with my parents and wouldn't need it for a while. So we were literally renting a storage unit to hold all the stuff we owned but wouldn't actually use.

After that, we moved every two years for a decade, which helped keep the belongings we owned down, because each move involved a "clean out" and donation spree of stuff we acquired but then a few short years later found we didn't need anymore.

Fifteen years after that student called me out, our family would move again, this time from Chicago to Denver, where I had accepted a new role, the kind of opportunity that gets you to move your family across the country. We had lived in our rental house in Chicago for six years, starting the year our third child was born. So we had a mountain of baby gear even though the "baby" was almost six years old.

It was the beginning of the Marie Kondo craze, and I was attracted to her simple idea: only keep the things that bring you joy. If you aren't familiar with Kondo's book *The Life-Changing Magic of Tidying Up*, it guides you to take an entire category of your belongings all at once (starting with clothes, or books, or kitchen items) and do a critical examination of whether the item still brings you joy. If it does, keep it, and if it doesn't, get rid of it. KonMari prescribes a specific way of then arranging the items you keep, including clothes, to help you be able to see and use the things you choose to own, which should be significantly fewer if you have done a ruthless job of clearing the clutter. Importantly, the KonMari method helps you let go of possessions that no longer bring joy by "thanking them" for their service, maybe photographing them, and finding them a good home.

I started with my clothes and whittled out bags and bags full. I folded the rest like she instructed so that my socks wouldn't be unhappy and my jeans stood up on one end. I moved on to our baby items and found much to dispose of at a local charity that would give them to mothers in need. I donated blankets and pillows and old towels to an animal shelter. I cleared out the knickknacks that no longer felt special, leaving room for the items that my husband, Billy, and I brought back from a summer teaching English in China in 1999, and for the great set of professional family photos taken in the Ogilvie train station a few summers before.

Simplify Your Life

What's important about the KonMari Method isn't the system for organizing the things you own; it's the conscious choice of what to own in the first place, the mentality of focusing on what brings you joy and eliminating the rest. The simplicity that remains is easier to organize and keep neat, but it's also easier on your mind having fewer possessions to remember, care for, and organize.

The lightness of removing the junk from my house couldn't be overstated. It's stuck with me, this idea of removing the belongings that don't bring me joy. But while the initial experience focused on removing items I already owned, I've since focused on not accumulating new possessions that aren't necessary, that won't bring me joy over time. Most objects I can look at and already see myself donating to a thrift store six months later: plastic toys for the kids, specialized kitchen gadgets, souvenir T-shirts, another eye shadow or the latest nail polish, those trendy jeans. So instead, I just don't buy them. Which is perhaps the most important aspect of reducing your footprint: don't buy what you don't truly need.

I'm not saying my purchase habits are pristine. Three months ago I bought a faux leather jacket from Zara "for work" that I haven't quite found the occasion to wear yet. But evaluating our discretionary spending history for the last few months, it's highly concentrated on food (I love a great meal), experiences (going to see family once we were vaxxed and felt safe traveling), and services (haircuts, carpet cleaning, vet bills).

We definitely buy stuff when we need it (growing kids, yadda yadda yadda), but one practice we don't do is shop as a form of entertainment. It's easy in American culture to get to the point where consumption becomes a mindless habit, a way to entertain ourselves on a Saturday with nothing else going on. *To live an integrated life, consumption has to be viewed as a purposeful choice.*

Everybody can recite the mantra "reduce, reuse, recycle." But we tend to skip over that first part, "reduce." It comes first in the saying for a reason—it's the most fundamental change we can make to our mindset and the way we live.

I have simplified and reduced nonphysical items as well, like running. I used to run a few miles a few times a week, at a very middling pace. I didn't enjoy it but felt obligated to get that exercise. I would walk frequently in the middle of my "runs," in deference to my lungs rather than my legs. I forced myself to complete a half marathon in 2011, on the tenth anniversary of 9/11, as a fundraiser for a beloved charity and also to "take back" my 9/11 birthday as a positive day of accomplishment. But I hated every minute of the actual running.

Eventually I realized I liked the walking parts a lot better. I could breathe, I could listen to a podcast without my earbuds falling out, and I still got exercise and fresh air without my knees complaining so much. The day I gave up running was a day of great joy. I let it go. I let that activity go but also the identity of being a "runner." I made peace with the idea that I wasn't that person who runs for fun and logs a hundred miles each month. And now instead of feeling an obligation to run and being miserable throughout it, I look forward to walking and enjoy every step.

I tell this story to point out that the concept of walking lightly in the world relates to your entire lifestyle. Beyond possessions, as you evaluate your life, what are the activities that aren't bringing you joy? What are the relationships that aren't bringing you joy? What are the habits and ways of being in the world that aren't bringing you joy? What are the expectations laid on you by the Current that aren't bringing you joy? It's okay to lay those things down and not pick them up again.

Adopting the Purchasing Hierarchy to Reduce Consumption

Many sources that are telling you to make ethical choices for consumption are still telling you to consume stuff you don't need. *Here, buy this organic cotton sweater. Here, buy this ethically sourced faux-leather handbag. Here, buy this jewelry with conflict-free diamonds.* But for me, buying stuff, even when it is ethically produced, is still consumption and is not ideal. We are not going to buy our way out of the mess we have created for this planet.

My formula for consumption choices is:

- Do I really need it? Can I make do with something I already have?

- If I really need it, do I need to own it? Will my use of this item be long term and frequent? If not, can I borrow it instead?

- If I can't borrow it, can I get it gently used?

- If I can't get it gently used, can I get it new from an ethically produced, sustainable source?

- If I can't get it from a sustainable source, can I get a high-quality product so that it will last?

Everything has become disposable, from paper towels and napkins and silverware to clothing, cell phones, and refrigerators. And if not outright disposable, then made of plastic that never decomposes and is much harder to recycle than industry would like you to think. Adopting the purchasing hierarchy helps you shrink your own footprint so you aren't contributing so much to the consumption of natural resources or to the landfills.

REDUCE, REUSE, *REPAIR*, REPLACE

Recently when our microwave started acting up, we were faced with that age-old dilemma: it would be $400 to fix it, or $500 to just buy a new one. Maybe the economically "smart" thing to do is get a new one, with a new warranty, and just throw the old one away. That's certainly what the repair technician encouraged me to do. But I can't. I'd rather repair than replace items, especially when there isn't a thrift center or a recycling option; that microwave would just go to the dump. That doesn't sit right with me, so I paid the $400 to have it repaired.

In that common saying "reduce, reuse, recycle," some people add a fourth: repair. Viewing your possessions as long-term investments means sometimes you pay for a repair rather than replacing it for the same cost. It means you have the button sewed back on those pants or the heel replaced on that shoe. It means keeping your cell phone as long as it works—and replacing that slow battery or clearing the junk if you can, rather than automatically upgrading to the newest version to gain 0.06 seconds of processing speed.

Know Where It Goes

Reducing what we purchase and seeking out ethically sourced suppliers is all about what happens *before* we make a purchase. But the other end of the equation is what happens *after* that purchase has outlived its usefulness.

In manufacturing, "throughput" refers to the amount of material that passes through a system. What is the throughput of your lifestyle? The corollary of "consume less" is to think about how to dispose of the items you do acquire.

I'm not saying you should own only five pieces of clothing or keep the same furniture for your entire adult life. Sometimes you need to follow "out with the old and in with the new." But when we casually say, "Out with the old," where does that old stuff go?

Many people take unwanted items to charitable organizations that run thrift stores, like Goodwill, Salvation Army, or others. But I encourage you *not* to do that unless you have no other options. There are a few reasons behind this recommendation, which may be counterintuitive.

Charity thrift stores serve many great purposes, but in some ways they make this particular problem worse—first, because they throw away or sell off most of what they receive to wholesale recyclers for a few pennies per pound. Experts estimate that thrift stores get rid of 90 percent of the clothing donated in this way.[8] That donated clothing goes to one of two places: it's dumped overseas on developing economies for super cheap (and charity experts agree that this is bad for those developing economies), or it's recycled into rags, insulation, or other nonclothing uses. This is not ideal because clothing should be used as clothing—that's a higher-level use than rags. You don't want it broken down into rags if it's still useful as clothing.

But here's the other way that donating clothing and other goods to thrift stores makes the problem worse: it just gets it out of our house and out of our sight, and we tell ourselves that we've done something good. It's not so bad that we're buying way more cheap stuff than we need, because when we're tired of it we're donating it to charity and someone will be glad to have it, right? Wrong. There is far more clothing and housewares discarded than anyone wants or needs. Charity thrift stores have the same impact as off-shore manufacturing: they provide the illusion of a clean and tidy ecosystem and a responsible consumer economy. If we no longer had the option to donate our unwanted stuff, we would have to face up to our own overconsumption.

If the money that might come from selling items would be useful to you (and worth the time and effort), consider selling your unwanted stuff on craigslist, eBay, or a local forum. But even if you don't need the money, it might be eye-opening to you to work with a reseller who will be discerning about what people actually want. They may reject 75 percent of your items because they aren't in good enough condition. Charity thrift stores view disposing of your unsellable junk as part of their business model—they can afford to sift through for the 10 percent of good stuff because their cost basis for all of the donated goods they resell is $0. That gives them the wiggle room to pay for the labor and lose 90 percent of donated items to disposal or recycling and still come out ahead. But those working for profit and buying stuff from you won't do your dirty work for you; they'll let you know something is not good enough for resale and force you to face your own consumption.

If you want some kind of tax deduction (and if your clothing is truly beat up because your three-year-old wore holes in all the knees and there are grape juice stains on half the shirts), then take it to Goodwill—they'll recycle it, and that's great. But if your items are still usable, try to find a smaller charity that will give the items to people in need rather than recycle or junk them just because they can't handle the volume.

If you don't care about getting a tax deduction or getting money, consider offering it for free to someone who wants it. Find a local "freecycle" group, ask your neighbors and friends if anyone can use it, or find a pet shelter or women's shelter that needs the items. If we care about what happens to the stuff we no longer need, we become more aware of how much we are buying and consuming, and it helps us to be better conservationists.

To walk more lightly in the world, reduce the number of things you buy, make the goods you buy last longer, and then try to pass them on or dispose of them thoughtfully when you no longer need them.

CHAPTER 7

Know Your Power

Have you ever been super sick and felt just drained? Unable to move, unable to accomplish anything, just drained. Maybe it took all your energy to get yourself from the bed to the couch to have some soup from a can for lunch. Or you had a headache that stuck with you for hours or days, making it hard to focus or accomplish anything.[1]

And then when you recover, you have a spring in your step. Feeling at full strength now feels like *more* than full strength. The absence of pain is exhilarating, leaving you on top of the world. As someone who has suffered from my share of intense headaches, I know how that feels. As you feel the headache lifting, you feel almost giddy with the prospect of living at full strength!

What if I told you that today most people are operating like they have a migraine when it comes to using their full selves for a better world. That they are weighed down and only using 5 percent of their power. What if I could multiply the power you have available to live out your values in search of a better world?

You might be thinking, "I have a very modest charity budget. I can't do much to change the world with the small amount I give to charities." And you're right: when you limit your impact power to thinking only of the money you have to give to charity, you're operating at 5 percent battery power.

So where do you get the other 95 percent? Let's do an inventory of the full assets that you have at your disposal, even if you live modestly:

- You spend money to maintain your household, including buying food (raw or prepared), furniture, cleaning supplies, utilities, decorations, and everyday essentials. You may also pay for upkeep services like lawn care or housekeeping.

- You probably spend money on clothing for yourself and other family members.

- You may have children and pay for their care, education, and extracurricular activities.

- You spend money on entertainment, including your internet, television, music, movies, cell phones and apps, theater, and art.

- You spend money on transportation, including a car, insurance, gas, bicycles, buses, planes, trains, and automobiles. You may travel for work or for vacation.

- You probably have a bank account, credit cards, hopefully health insurance, life insurance, and maybe even a 401(k) or brokerage account, even if the balances are small.

- You may have discretionary income that you can spend as you like.

In total, your household might have tens of thousands of dollars moving through it every year—maybe more! But beyond a checkbook, you have other important assets:

- You have a network of friends, neighbors, and acquaintances—people with whom you have social capital.

- You may have professional skills and experience and a working environment that includes coworkers and potentially customers or clients.

- Are you a business owner? You have employees, vendors, customers, and community, and you may have products at cost.

- You probably have at least some free time.

- You undoubtedly have talents, whether it's communicating with strangers, creative pursuits, playing poker, singing, dancing, or cross-stitching.

- You may have access to a flexible space inside or outside your home.

- You may also have access to influential people and networks, like an alumni group, a collection of former colleagues, or influential leaders in the community, other parents at your kids' school or from their extracurricular activities.

- You may also have various forms of privilege that allow you to move through certain spaces more easily than others. Privilege comes in many forms, from being seen as white, being seen as attractive, being tall, being male, being straight, being married and being Christian, being neurotypical with no visible disabilities, and a native-born citizen of the United States. You may have some of these characteristics and not others, but each one provides a certain level of access and deference that is an asset and an advantage, whether you consciously decide to use it or not.

With this inventory in mind, can you start to see how many levers for change are at your disposal? How many choices you make every day? It makes me feel powerful to realize how much I have at my disposal.

Look back at that list now and find one bullet that you hadn't considered before. Better yet, put a star or a check beside all the bullets that apply to you and your life. In Part II, we tackle all these different areas and talk about how you can activate them in service of shared prosperity. But for now, simply take inventory. Take note of the many forms of power and influence you have when you put everything on the table. No sacred cows here, no off-limits areas of your life. That's the challenge and the pain and the reward of trying to lead an integrated life. Rather than walling off some (usually financial) area of your life where you're willing to compromise your values in service to your personal interests, you keep poking and *be brave*, saying, "How can I do better?"

Individual action is nice, and *necessary*, but let me be clear that it is not *sufficient* without collective action—in other words, without public policy.

Volunteering Is Nice; Voting Is Essential

I don't know about you, but sometimes I find it's easier to be friendly and kind to random strangers and neglectful of relationships close to home. But community—a physical, actual neighborhood community—is an incredibly important factor in quality of life for us and others around us. There is much joy to be had from building authentic relationships with your neighbors, people with whom you may have loose social connections. I have the most wonderful neighbors on my block—committed parents (including dog and cat parents) and individuals who say hi and smile when walking the dogs, who open their windows so we can enjoy the piano playing, who gladly offer advice to a neighbor who sliced her finger pretty good and thinks it looks a little green a few days later and is wondering if she should go back to urgent care to have it looked at. Neighbors who look out for one another and one another's kids and who are a fun group to sit with in a giant, socially distanced circle in the alley during a pandemic.

The first step beyond yourself is to show up in the broader community of which you are a member—your geographic community. Volunteering to help our community is a natural act for many of us. And it should be commended and appreciated. But it's not enough.

I've served on a dozen nonprofit boards. But one thing you learn in philanthropy is that private actors (like nonprofits, foundations, donors, and even businesses) are absolutely tiny in comparison to the impact of government. Here are a few examples of what I mean:

- You can volunteer at your kid's school and influence their love of reading and help support individual kids. But your local school district sets policy about things like curriculum, teacher pay, class sizes, facilities investments, and transportation issues that dramatically affect thousands or tens of thousands of children across their entire twelve years of elementary, middle, and high school.

- You can volunteer at a homeless shelter, serving meals and bringing comfort to unhoused neighbors, but your local government sets policy on zoning for affordable and multifamily housing, oversees police department budgets and policies, establishes drug courts, and authorizes mental health service providers to answer nonviolent 911 calls, suspends or upholds housing eviction policies and procedures and many other issues that affect people who lose their homes.

- You can be an individual mentor to a young transgender student to help them feel accepted and loved, but your state government may set policy about whether that student can receive gender-affirming medical care before they turn eighteen.

- You can turn off the water while brushing your teeth, but your county may have the power to maintain water lines and set conditions to approve oil and gas permits that may threaten the local watershed and your safe drinking water.

I'm not saying you shouldn't volunteer in your community or that volunteering and private philanthropy are not good activities. They are good and noble. But they aren't solutions, and they aren't a replacement for government policy. *We cannot solve these problems as individuals and through individual choices.* This is a "yes, *and*" situation—we have to make different personal choices, *and* we have to use the enormous power of government to bring about change in industry that is not optional and long term but demands action now.

I once posted on social media that I had to cast a provisional ballot because I hadn't voted since the last presidential election. And wasn't that ridiculous, I said; I had only missed a few *local* elections! Well, a friend took me to task, pointing out how important local elections are to our everyday lives—probably more important than presidential elections. Local elected officials have influence over public safety, police and school budgets, local taxes, and infrastructure spending. They also have a great deal of control over the way elections themselves are conducted, which means that whether the next presidential election is free and fair will be greatly influenced by who wins those "in-between" elections.

So if you want to go beyond your personal conscience ("I'm not contributing to this problem with my personal actions") to solving the problems we face, you must get involved and vote for elected officials who will turn your values into laws—or run for office yourself!

Educate yourself about local prosecutors, judges, and school board candidates. Stay informed and engaged with local news sources—subscribe and support them financially if you can, and listen to public radio if you can't. Follow journalists and elected officials on social media. Show up for civic celebrations and protest marches alike. Yes, volunteer in your community to help your neighbors. And above all, *vote*. Every election, every issue.

Your Actions Matter

I hope you now fully realize that you have many assets—money you spend, relationships and talents you nurture, voting, volunteering—that you can use to help further the cause of shared prosperity in this world. But none of these assets will do any good unless you take action.

Some people tell me that they feel helpless because they can't fix the global issues we face. There's no doubt that the world currently finds itself in a pretty deep hole. And it's true that a few thousand individuals avoiding plastic straws won't do much to reduce the amount of plastics found in the ocean. Volunteering at a food bank won't solve the problem of hunger in America. Nonetheless, as they say, "If you find yourself in a hole, stop digging." Part of your power is to stop contributing to the problems you see and start being part of the solution.

I also believe in the collective power of individual action. Can you imagine how incredibly powerful you could be if your everyday choices were clearly aligned with your values and working toward a better world? And then if everyone around you did it too? Imagine everyone fully powered on. You'd shine out like a lighthouse and be surrounded by others' light, and the light of the community would grow and grow. That's what the integrated life can feel like. That's what we're chasing, together.

PART II

Action Steps

It's not who you are underneath; it's what you do that defines you.

—RACHEL DAWES, *BATMAN BEGINS*

I told you when we started this that I wasn't going to give you rules—and it's true, I'm not. *My* rules probably wouldn't work for you. Partially because I live a different life, and partially because I have my own ranking of the importance of issues like global warming, worker rights, animal rights, and so on, that may be slightly different from yours. But I am going to try to help you set your own rules that reflect your dedication to an integrated life.

Why do you even need rules, you may ask? Why not just have a general attitude of "try to do better"? Because, to quote my small Jedi friend, "Do, or do not. There is no *try*." At the root, to stick with a new habit, we must believe it is a part of our identity and who we are, not just something we try to do now and then.

By creating rules for yourself, you are saying, "This is who I am," and you remove the decision fatigue associated with making many decisions over and over. For example, when I met a friend recently for happy hour, we ordered a chef's board to share. When it arrived, I told him, "The olives are all yours; I don't eat olives," and he told me, "That prosciutto is all yours; I don't eat pork." Personally, I was just motivated by taste, as I think olives and mushrooms have the same disgusting texture and I can't stand to bite into them. But he was motivated by something else—he'd been a consultant to a meat processor, and after observing the process, the working conditions, and the treatment of animals, he decided he wasn't a person who supported the pork industry and cut it out of his diet.

Notice that neither one of us said, "I *try* not to eat this food," which suggests you might change your mind at some point in the future. Rather, we each said, "I *don't* eat this food," which is a strong, declarative sentence about who we are—and is not up for negotiation.

Setting your own boundaries and drawing a line in the sand that you won't cross makes it easier to deal with situations where you might otherwise have to make a choice. Consider the difference between "I'm a pacifist" and "I try not to punch people." Or "I'm trying to drink less" and "I don't drink during the workweek."

How about "I try to take my bike when I can" and "I bike instead of drive to any destination closer than five miles."

As you read the chapters that follow, I encourage you to find your own line in the sand. To not just settle for "I'll try" but to develop some rules for yourself that correspond to who you are and what you believe in.

That said, I encourage you to take small steps and tackle one area at a time. In each chapter, I try to start with a minimal commitment and move to greater and greater commitments of time, energy, or money. You may find that the first level of commitment is all you can manage right now. That's fine. Start there, but start firm with a commitment that reflects your identity as someone who believes in shared prosperity for all people and the planet we call home. And then over time, as you feel the psychological benefits of alignment more strongly, you can take another step. And the next one after that. And keep on doing the next right thing.

If you are ready for more steps, more reflection, and more opportunities to find community with others paddling away from the mainstream, come join us at www.theintegratedlife.com.

CHAPTER 8

Food: Being Mindful of What You Eat (and Where It Comes From)

Eat [real] food, not too much, mostly plants.

—MICHAEL POLLAN, *IN DEFENSE OF FOOD:*
AN EATER'S MANIFESTO

Let's start by talking about food. Everyone needs it, everyone has to spend money on it, and so it's an area where everyone makes choices every day. Many times, those choices have unclear consequences. Remember that tomato from the TV series *The Good Place*? I don't want you to be caught in analysis paralysis, wondering if your food choices are going to send you to the Bad

Place. But most of us have much room for growth and improvement in our food choices.

Food from Organic and Regenerative Agriculture

One of the most powerful trends in eating is making sure that the choices we make about what food we buy and consume does the least harm to the world around us—meaning both the physical environment and the humans who grow, harvest, and process the food. But going beyond sustainable food that doesn't make things worse, we must move toward regenerative practices that actively repair and heal the damage to the world.

Most people today are aware of *organic agriculture*, which involves a number of nature-friendly practices, the most important of which may be avoiding the use of harmful chemicals on the crops. This matters because those chemicals have multiple negative effects on people and the environment. For example, chemicals often wash into the water supply as water used to grow crops soaks into the ground. Those same chemicals can also wash into rivers and streams when it rains, affecting marine life and water quality for human consumption. The people who plant, tend, and harvest the fruits and vegetables can also suffer health problems when man-made pesticides and herbicides are used. Finally, you and I can also be negatively affected by eating chemical residue found in or on our food.

Why would farmers use such harmful chemicals, you may wonder? A few reasons: they can repel common bugs that might otherwise eat the plants, as well as prevent or cure diseases that can ruin the whole field if left unchecked. Which is why pesticides are useful inventions. Unfortunately, they also stress out the soil, as do many modern farming practices, like planting the same crop over and over. Different crops have different profiles in terms of what they extract or replace in the soil. So planting the same crop over and over will deplete those nutrients. As soil becomes stripped of its natural nutrients, farmers have to replace those nutrients with more and more artificial fertilizers to help those same crops grow.

Some of these problems are self-imposed by consumers—we think we prefer pretty, plump, and large produce, helped along with chemical fertilizers. But have you ever noticed that the visually flawless, giant apple is less flavorful? Scientists have found today's apples (and other kinds of produce) contain only 50 percent of the nutrients of produce grown fifty years ago.[1] At the same time, the plants have become weaker and need more protection in the form of more bug repellant and disease prevention. It's a downward spiral, increasing the need for stronger and stronger chemicals, resulting in blander and weaker food.

Organic agriculture seeks to reverse this trend. It seeks to naturally grow crops that are suited to the soil, eliminating or at least minimizing the use of chemical pesticides and fertilizers.

Regenerative agriculture refers to farming practices that seek to naturally restore nutrients to the soil by (among other practices) rotating native crops, which are those that developed naturally in the area and are therefore more resistant to local pests and disease. As the novel coronavirus showed us, human diseases flourish when they can travel to new species/locations and take over unsuspecting and unprepared populations. It works the same way with plant diseases. Agricultural crop varieties introduced to a new location can be quite susceptible to local diseases and insects. But plants that have been cultivated in an area for a long time tend to develop defenses. The reverse is also true: foreign (non-native) invasive crop species, insects, and diseases can wreak havoc on local crops that have no defense against them.

For all these reasons, buying organic produce is a common choice for people who value the environment. If you feel like organic produce is a little more expensive than you can afford, consider starting with the "Dirty Dozen," the conventional produce containing the most pesticide residue (even after being washed and peeled), as highlighted by the Environmental Working Group based on extensive testing by the Food and Drug Administration.[2]

But becoming a certified organic farmer is an expensive and time-consuming process; "organic" is a term that is regulated by the federal government, and you can't call your produce organic unless it meets the standards for that label. One thing to note is that many small farmers can't afford the time and money to achieve that certification, although they may adopt many of the practices of organic farming.

The practical barriers to becoming an organic food producer are what drive many others to invoke principle 5: *resist the allure of convenience*, and shop local for food as much as you can. If you can see and talk to the farmers who grow your food—say, at a farmer's market or a local farm stand—you have the ability to ask about their cultivation practices and why they may not be certified organic. If they are committed to organic or regenerative agricultural practices, they likely grow heritage varieties of popular produce such as tomatoes, corn, apples, and greens.

When you buy local food, you are also supporting more sustainable practices because the food grown in season requires fewer resources—less fertilizer, water, or artificial sun. Buying tomatoes year-round may be appealing to our Taco Tuesday tradition, but it does have a much greater environmental impact than those summer heritage tomatoes from the farmer's market.

Another benefit of buying food grown locally is that there is often a smaller footprint from transportation, helping you to *walk lightly in the world*. If your blueberries say, "Product of Chile," you are holding something that has traveled a long way and consumed a great deal of fuel and other resources to arrive at your local supermarket. I'm not going to tell you to never eat blueberries again, but if you have a choice, choose a local producer.

Additionally, buying from local producers keeps wealth and jobs in your community. Being a farmer is tough, backbreaking, and often poorly paying work. Being a farmworker even more so. The prices from local produce are probably lower because of the transportation savings, but the impact is even greater when you keep wealth circulating in your own community. If you can afford it, paying a little more at the farmer's market for local and/ or organic produce is another way to *just give*.

Buying Food from a Grocery Story

If only the food itself could be magically delivered into our cupboards and refrigerators. For most of us, we still have to go to the grocery store to buy food and bring it home. A few thoughts about grocery stores.

First, try not to contribute to the 40 percent of food that is wasted.[3] Help the store save on food waste by being open to buying ugly or imperfect produce. Once these items are diced up and in your dish, no one will know it was once a crooked cucumber or gnarled red pepper. If you're like me, the bigger problem is that you buy some strawberries without a plan to use them, and they go bad in your refrigerator. I highly recommend you start some simple meal planning to make sure you don't buy perishables that you won't use.

Second, take steps to minimize the use of plastics. Grocery stores use plastic like their profits depend on it. You would think they are in the plastic business instead of the food business, and maybe they are. But the constant push toward plastic is, to me, incredibly painful. If you buy organic produce but put it in a thin plastic bag, which then gets packed at checkout into another plastic bag, are you environmentally neutral, at best? I highly encourage you to use those reusable grocery bags that are probably in your house right now. If you're like most people, you have five (or more!) of them scattered around but never when you need them. That used to be me, too. Let me tell you how I got into a routine that has drastically reduced the amount of plastic I use and improved my family's grocery footprint.

When the pandemic hit hard in March of 2020, I took the role of "executive chef" within my household. That means I was in charge of menu planning, procuring ingredients, making meals, and keeping the pantry and fridge stocked with staples. My goal was to have a single, weekly grocery run and otherwise avoid the crowds (and germs). Because I had access to a local food co-op, a Sunday farmer's market, and a grocery store, I try to pay a little "convenience tax" in order to shop local and *just give*. My standard practice became:

- Review and select recipes for the week ahead with my family on Saturday afternoon and use that to create a detailed shopping list (then check my pantry to confirm what I already have on hand and cross that off the list).

- Go online to place an order with my local food co-op for delivery.

- On Sunday morning, grab my reusable bags of various sizes and head out to the farmer's market first (those months when it was open) and then the grocery store.

This simple routine has helped my family greatly increase the amount of locally grown food we use and reduce the packaging when we need to buy more conventional items. (You can find more detail about my routine on my website, www.theintegratedlife.com, and even find instructions for a thirty-day challenge if you want to try improving your grocery store practices.)

Does it matter what grocery store you shop at? What if you are more focused on fair labor practices and want to prioritize that value over or alongside environmental impact? There is a significant difference between different grocery store chains (and independent stores) and how they treat their workers. We all found during the pandemic how critical our grocery store workers are, and yet groceries can be a very low-margin business. Low margins are often used as an excuse to keep wages low and deny people full-time hours and therefore benefits, or to fail to offer any employees key benefits like health insurance or paid time off. I am not an expert on the grocery/farming business, but I do think it's worth keeping labor practices in mind while considering what store to shop at.[4]

Being More Responsible When Eating Out

The restaurant business is a critical part of the small business community. According to the National Restaurant Association, even with the impacts of the pandemic, in 2020 restaurants brought in $659 billion in sales and employed 12.5 million workers (down 3.1 million from expected levels because of pandemic closures).[5] Seven in ten restaurants are single-unit operations, which means they are small businesses where the owners probably work long hours every day. Many local communities have rallied around their restaurants in an attempt to keep these locally owned, family businesses alive and thriving. Even if you're limiting your budget for eating out, consider the following factors for the few times that you do get a chef-created meal.

TAKEOUT

During the pandemic, many restaurants had no outdoor dining options, which meant everything was in a take-out container. I am not actually allergic to it, but the sight of Styrofoam makes me feel a little ill. It's one of those convenience items that we just throw away—and it lives forever and ever in a landfill. More environmentally conscious restaurants use compostable or at least recyclable containers. If you get those, take the extra minute to scrape out any remaining food and then recycle or compost them. And don't let them give you single-use plastic silverware and cups and extras. Use real silverware when you get home.

SOURCING

Does the restaurant source from local farms and producers? This is important for all the same reasons you want to source locally for your own food and supplies, multiplied by one hundred, since they feed one hundred times more people than you and use way more ingredients. Check the restaurant website before visiting—they will often talk about their sourcing partners.

FAIR LABOR PRACTICES

Do they have a toxic kitchen culture? Do they have any females in leadership? This might be hard to tell, but if the place seems to have high turnover in their wait staff every time you visit, they may not be treating people well.

TIPPING

In the case of restaurant workers, remember to *just give*! These days 20 percent is the minimum tip for even a take-out order, and 25 percent for eating in. As a reminder, those extra few dollars from you add up and make a huge difference for someone living on minimum wage and tips.

I have to admit that having been a server for a few years in college makes me both more understanding and more critical at the same time. I used to leave the server a tip according to the perceived level of service—15 percent is standard, right? So you had to be really great to get a 20 percent tip. This felt judicious and reasonable and fair.

But since the 2008 recession, I started to think differently about tipping service people of all kinds. I kept hearing stories about how people were eating out less, getting their hair cut less, certainly vacationing less. And it seems like the people most affected by this are the people who can afford it the least.

Servers, for example, make far less than minimum wage, usually no more than $3 or $4 an hour. Instead of hourly wages, tips make up the bulk of their income. When I was a server, I could take home the tips I made in cash each day, and I felt lucky if the hourly wages paid by the restaurant covered my taxes due for the period.

Despite the recession and the most recent pandemic, I'm still able to eat out with my family. I'm still getting my hair cut, and now I'm back to taking a Lyft and traveling regularly for work. I view these interactions as opportunities to help out the people working hard every day and probably taking home less than they used to, through no fault of their own. To help compensate for fewer customers with tighter purse strings, I've become an "overtipper": 20 percent is now my minimum tip for servers and hairdressers and the like. An extra few bucks can make a big difference to these people.

And even if I use a credit or debit card to pay for the service, I try to tip in cash so the service person can have it immediately to take home. It's more flexible for them, and they may need the cash flow, rather than waiting for the company to put credit card tips into their next paycheck.

JOIN OVERTIPPERS ANONYMOUS!

I'm also more mindful of tipping the various people I run into during my business travels: hotel doormen who get my luggage (even if I could do it myself) and housekeepers who clean the room ($5 per night, left on the nightstand).

Beyond the people you tip each time they provide a service, many etiquette writers suggest you tip folks during the holidays as a way to say "thanks" for great service throughout the year. I give $20 for the paper delivery and milk delivery folks, $20 for the trash collectors, and for the mail carrier. An extra tip for your babysitter or hair stylist.

So if you'd like to join my new club, "Overtippers Anonymous," be warned: it's not a #lifehack to save a few bucks. But instead of feeling judicious (which I view in a completely different way, now seeing how close it is to "judgmental"), you'll feel gratitude, solidarity, and joy when you *just give*.

Reflect Your Values through Other Eating Choices

Besides paying more attention to what you buy from grocery stores and restaurants, there are many other changes you can make that will help you *walk lightly* when it comes to your food choices. Here are a few ideas to get you started.

GROW YOUR OWN FOOD

If you really want a gold star, considering growing a Victory Garden with your own tomatoes, peppers, or herbs. You'll enjoy fresh food, no pesticides, and no transportation costs to you or the environment, plus a healthy hobby that gets you outside.

If do you start a garden or already have one, I bet you have had the experience of having too many tomatoes to possibly eat. Maybe you found zucchini easy to grow but your family doesn't love it. I've had generous neighbors offer me fresh basil from their garden many times. Have you ever considered donating some portion of your bounty to the local food pantry? There are a number of programs that facilitate the donation of extra produce in communities; try searching for "grow a row" in your town.

START A COMPOSTING SYSTEM (TO FEED THAT GARDEN)

My family tried to have a large compost bin in our back-yard when we lived in Chicago, and truthfully it was too unwieldy, and I didn't really know how to manage it: food

---

scraps went in, but useful fertilizer never came out. Now in Denver, our backyard is too small for a composting bin, even if we wanted it. Instead, we have a stainless steel bucket with an odor-absorbing lid, about the size of a bathroom trash can. It lives under the stove in our kitchen, fitted with a compostable liner held in place by a large rubber band. When it gets full, we pull out the bag, bunch the sides to tie it up, and walk it down to our neighbor's composting bin. We fill it every few days, and I am so glad those food scraps are going to be composted instead of going into a landfill.

A few years back, we bought an indoor composting system powered by worms. Yes, real live worms lived in my kitchen, nestled down in a bed of newspaper scraps, cardboard, egg shells, coconut fibers, and paper towels. Every few days my kids and I would feed them a few hands full of kitchen scraps, including coffee grounds, apple cores, the bits of broccoli I trimmed off, and the tops of all those strawberries we bought at the farmer's market. Inside my clean, odorless bin, the worms were turning the scraps into compost that would feed our garden. If this sounds fun for your family (and especially if you have kids), search online for "urban worms" (or "vermicomposting," if you're feeling fancy). You can find many tutorials and supply companies to help you get started. It's not gross (I swear), but it's not for everyone.

START MEAL PLANNING

Meal planning is an important part of our food choices so we don't end up making spur-of-the-moment decisions about eating fast food or ordering takeout, or waste food that goes unused until it is inedible. (It also helps me avoid a situation where I feel like I'm competing on a home-grown episode of *Chopped* and have to make a meal out of four random ingredients in the produce drawer. I would definitely lose on *Chopped*.) Planning how we'll use food also has a positive impact on the amount of food waste we generate: it helps us avoid having that lettuce rot or the zucchini get mushy before we manage to use it in something.

To get started with meal planning, make a list somewhere of your go-to meals that come up frequently and the ingredients they require. Add one or two new recipes each week so you don't get bored. And don't forget to take into account the nights where no one has time to cook by including a crockpot recipe or two that you can start in the morning and just finish with one or two easy steps when you're ready to eat. Or a night to eat those leftovers before they spoil in the back of the fridge.

PICK YOUR OWN PRODUCE

One way small farmers supplement their income is by inviting the public to pick their own produce. Our little family has often enjoyed a hayride out to the field, the satisfaction of finding the perfect strawberry/blueberry/apple/pumpkin, petting the farm animals, and a lunch that usually involves hot dogs, as well as farm-made treats like apple cider or muffins and pies. PickYourOwn.org provides a helpful search tool (http://www.pickyourown.org/index .htm#states) that you can use to find a "pick your own" farm near you.

When we lived in Chicago, every year we visited a farm where we could pick our own strawberries for Father's Day, and we filled up two huge baskets and turned it into freezer jam. The fruit is usually sold by weight, and you're paying for the experience as well as the produce, but if you'll eat it, can it, freeze it, or share it, it's still a good deal and a good time. Plus, your kids will get a kick out of seeing the farm, eating a few berries right off the vine or apples right off the tree (which the farm usually expects and encourages, to a reasonable degree), and it's a whole day of family entertainment.

BUY A SEASON'S WORTH OF PRODUCE FROM A LOCAL FARMER

This concept is called community-supported agriculture, or CSA. The idea is that you find a farm nearby and sign up as a shareholder at the beginning of the season.[6] Then each week your farmer will bring a box of whatever is ready to be picked. Usually the farm has a few local drop-off sites. The downside to this approach is that you pay for the whole season up front (easily $500). And I highly recommend you find a CSA that includes a list of what they're sending you and maybe a few recipes to use it; otherwise you might be stuck posting pictures of your box on social media with captions like, "Can anyone tell me what this is and how to cook it?" (I speak from experience here. If you're wondering, it was garlic scapes, but I still had no idea what to do with them.)

ADVOCATE AT YOUR KIDS' SCHOOL FOR SERVING HEALTHY, LOCAL FOOD

Most schools are just doing what's easy, what's affordable, and what's been arranged for them by the district or some other supervising force. But there are many companies working to make school lunches easy, affordable, *and* healthy, while supporting their local farmers and the local environment. Could you reach out to the school's parent organization and begin a conversation about switching from a provider whose menu includes some form of pizza every other day to a local organic food vendor?

Becoming a Vegetarian or Vegan

Whether we're driven by a desire to *walk lightly in the world*, a belief that animals shouldn't suffer in the name of human convenience, or simply health concerns, many of us are reconsidering our relationship with animal products—primarily, meat.

First, while high in protein, animal products have saturated fat and cholesterol that should be eaten sparingly. Yet, as reported by NPR in 2012, "[Americans] still eat more meat per person here than in almost any other country on the planet. Only the Luxembourgers eat more meat than we do."[7] The average American eats more than three times the global average of meat. According to Johns Hopkins University research, this high level of meat consumption is putting us at greater risk for a range of health problems, including heart disease, stroke, type 2 diabetes, obesity, certain cancers, and earlier death.[8]

Second, the animal farming industry has an upsetting history around the way it treats animals. Born and raised with just inches of space and in filthy, disease-prone conditions, meat production is optimized for human convenience and profit, not for the respect and humane treatment of the animals that eventually become our food.

Third, they also have a history of mistreating workers with long hours, lack of safety measures, and repetitive motions.[9] During the pandemic, meat processing plants were notorious for their COVID-19 outbreaks;[10] hundreds of workers would fall ill, and companies tried to avoid taking care of them or allowing them paid time off to recover or just to quarantine for everyone's safety.

Finally, eating meat is hard on the planet. Meat production is a major source of methane, a greenhouse gas that leads to global warming. Animal offal has been a source of pollution in local water sources. And meat production is also energy intensive: one to two liters of water is required to produce each calorie of fruits and vegetables, compared to ten liters for a single calorie of meat.[11]

If one or all of these reasons speaks to you and is a source of conflict between your values and your everyday choices, consider the following steps to reduce or eliminate the harm caused by your meat consumption.

BECOME A "FLEXITARIAN"

A flexitarian is someone who eats less meat but still leaves all options in their diet. You may have heard of Meatless Mondays, which is a great practice if you're just starting out. You could also opt to avoid meat at breakfast or lunch. Or save meat for the weekends or special days when you have time to cook. Make meat a special option instead of a daily habit. Flexitarians also replace some meat with seafood that is wild caught.

EAT MORE ETHICALLY PRODUCED MEAT

If you're like my husband and just crave a steak or some chicken wings now and then, you can still make beneficial changes to your meat sourcing. Is there a co-op or local producer where you could source the meat and other animal products (milk, eggs, cheese) you do eat? Like our eggs sourced from Farmer Gavin, our co-op works with small, local farms that grow their cattle without antibiotics or artificial hormones, gives them plenty of room to roam, and feeds them with regeneratively grown agriculture. If you don't have a co-op near you, does your grocery store offer ethically sourced meat?

You might also check out the meat and meal delivery companies that have won endorsement from the ASPCA's "Shop with Your Heart" program for their humane treatment of animals, including Butcher Box, Porter Road, Walden Local Meat Co., and others.[12] In addition, the Savory Institute in Boulder, Colorado, has developed a "land to market" certification, "the world's first verified regenerative sourcing solution for meat, dairy, wool & leather."[13] There you can find meat delivery boxes from folks like Rep Provisions (https://repprovisions.com), who are passionate about regenerative farming, soil health, and healing the planet.

STOP EATING MEAT ALTOGETHER

If you really want to *be brave*, go vegetarian! While most of our family is flexitarian, my oldest daughter is vegetarian, which has had a great impact on the rest of us in reducing our consumption. My advice if you want to give it a try is to invest in your own cooking skills and expand your recipe rotation. If you try to have the same meals but just skip the meat, you'll feel deprived, and the meals don't feel fulfilling. Instead, try dishes from cuisines that don't feature as much meat (that is, most cultures other than the United States).

To instill a sense of adventure around trying vegetarian dishes, every Sunday we try something new and a little more difficult, meaning it takes a few hours to make dinner as we learn a new technique. I've found three or four vegetable curry dishes I love, and in the last few years we've tried everything from samosas, egg rolls, pot stickers, spanakopita, and homemade pasta to roasted vegetable salads, Moroccan stews, and Mexican stuffed zucchini boats. Pinterest is your friend in this regard! Other nights, we stick to sixty minutes to get dinner on the table. (Sorry if this is a letdown, but there's no such thing as a thirty-minute meal; recipes labeled that way mean thirty minutes from the time you have all ingredients prepped and pan/stove heated, and so on.)

For the rest of the family, I'll include a meat component in dinner two or three nights a week. For example, we'll make a crockpot chili, and the meat eaters in the house can add in rotisserie chicken at the end. Same with gumbo and adding smoked sausage. Or we have hamburgers, and my daughter makes a black bean burger. Taken together, I like to think that my flexitarian family (and vegetarian daughter) don't feel deprived and maybe don't even notice when we sometimes go a whole week without any meat.

GO ALL THE WAY TO VEGAN

A vegan is someone who doesn't eat any animal products, including dairy, eggs, and even honey. If you want to try a vegan lifestyle, I have one piece of advice—don't swap meat for a whole bunch of meat substitutes or just for beans. Many vegan substitutes are hitting store shelves for everything from butter to burgers, but much of it is highly processed and not necessarily healthy. Don't try to re-create everything meat-like; instead cook dishes that revolve around vegetables and spices combined in interesting ways.

Change Your Eating Habits Gradually

Perhaps no habit (short of an addiction) is harder to change than what we eat—including where and how we obtain that food. My own family's journey toward more responsible eating has taken years. We have gradually expanded our standard menu of meals in part by experimenting with different cuisines and recipes. It took me some time to always remember to take my reusable grocery bags and mesh produce bags to the grocery store. Developing plans for what specific types of food I could purchase from different sources didn't happen overnight. And I still can't successfully grow a garden, or any plant, for that matter.

Be patient with yourself when it comes to changing your food shopping and eating habits. Pick one area and master that, and then gradually expand as your old habits are replaced by new ones. And if you'd like some more specific techniques and tips for what and how to eat more responsibly, head to www.theintegratedlife. com for a thirty-day challenge to jump-start your journey.

I expect that eating local, fresh foods is more expensive in some cases (organic definitely costs more) and cheaper in others (buying what's in season is cheaper and so is cooking instead of eating out). But even if my monthly grocery budget for our family of five went from $900 to $1,000, I consider that extra $100 per month an important part of using my consumer power to help bring about the world I want to see—one with a thriving local economy, healthier kids and a healthier me, fewer pesticides and other pollutants in the air and water, and more of a connection to where my food comes from. And I suspect that the message I'm sending to food companies with my choices each month will have a bigger impact on changing the world than a $100 donation to a charity working on the same issues.

CHAPTER 9

Clothing: Dress the Part

Clothes make the man. Naked people have
little or no influence on society.

—MARK TWAIN, *MORE MAXIMS OF MARK*

I have never been a fashionista, but like most of you, I've always
had to wear clothing in public. This is an area where we've been
trained to be consumers, to think of clothing as having a short life
span (at least while we own it), and then believe that it gets passed
on to another happy wearer via the charitable thrift shop. Clothing
companies want us to treat clothing as disposable so that we buy
more. Over time, the appetite for the latest fashion has sped up
more and more, leading to the creation of the fast fashion industry, which churns out disposable clothing in record time and for

incredibly low prices. Where people (Americans included) used to own relatively few items of clothing that were made to last, we now own dozens or even hundreds of outfits, and cycle through them with the seasons.

At least that's the model the fashion industry wants you to follow. It is also in their interest to have you believe that thrift stores are a good outlet for your unwanted clothing. Donate that bag to Goodwill, and some enterprising college kid will buy it and be thrilled with the "vintage" item. Or turn that cheap T-shirt back into the fast fashion place where you bought it, and they'll recycle it and give you a coupon off your next fast fashion purchase. Everyone wins, right? That's what I thought for many years.

But when I started researching the resale clothing business, I was horrified by what I found: only 10 percent of donated clothing is actually sold to another consumer; the rest ends up being recycled into rags, thrown away, or dumped in overseas markets.[1] Some of that is because such clothing is not fit to be anything more than rags. But a lot of it is because there is just too much to handle: *Slate* magazine reported that one—one!—Salvation Army distribution center in Brooklyn rejects eighteen tons of donated clothing every three days.[2] So the charities pick the best items and sell the rest in bulk for pennies on the pound. Their donors presumably don't know and don't care that it's trash or rags. They got the tax deduction and sense of doing a good deed and moved on to the next sweater, the next pair of jeans, the next cheap T-shirt.

In reality, we are producing much, much more clothing than we need, and at great cost to the people who make it and the environment that produces raw materials and ends up receiving unwanted throwaways and chemicals used in the production of our temporary wardrobes.[3]

The purchase hierarchy I described as part of principle 6 (*walk lightly*) was something I first developed in relation to clothes. Here's a quick reminder of the hierarchy, followed by some ideas on how to apply it to clothing:

1. Do I really need it?

2. Do I need to own it (or can I borrow or rent it)?

3. Can I get it gently used?

4. Can I get it new from an ethical, sustainable source?

5. Can I get a high-quality product that will last?

Do I Really Need It? Or Can I Make Do with Something I Already Have?

Unless you are Beyoncé walking the red carpet at the Met Gala, you *can* wear the same outfit twice. Maybe even dozens of times. Remember the Australian news anchor who wore the same blue suit on-screen every day for twelve months and nobody noticed?[4] Granted, he was a man, and women are held to a much, much different standard for fashionable clothing, but I think it's still safe to say other people aren't as into your clothes as you might think. So instead of assuming you need something new, this is the most important question you can ask yourself: "Do I truly need another pair of jeans or another sweater?" And if the answer is no, don't buy it.

Our economy depends on people buying stuff—and we often treat shopping as entertainment. I mean, why else would we go to the mall? But buying stuff we don't need is the root of the problem. "It takes 10,000 liters of water to produce one kilogram of cotton, meaning it takes about 2,700 liters to make 1 cotton T-shirt,"[5] and global cotton production requires over 250 billion tons of water annually. Though growing organic cotton uses significantly less water, it is not "good" for the world if you don't need the item it's made from. Your first choice, in order to *walk lightly in the world*, should be to pass up the garment altogether.

For me, this means I own seven pairs of shoes that I wear most days (black and brown work shoes, gray and brown boots, hiking boots, workout shoes, and white Adidas "dress" sneakers) and then a few pairs of heels that I rarely have to pull out. And I own about five pairs of jeans: black, gray, and dark blue skinny jeans, capri-length jeans with a hole in the knee, and the thick, large jeans I wear over leggings/long underwear when I'm headed outside in really cold weather. I haven't caught up to the latest trends in "mom jeans," which are a cruel joke of a *Saturday Night Live* skit come to life.[6]

A woman named Adrienne at my first job set this tone for me. She was my age and in the same role as me in another department. The foundation where we worked had a pretty formal dress code (this was the '90s, too, so everything was more formal then). We often had lunch together and attended meetings together. After a few months I realized that she wore the same suit every day. It was a beautiful black tailored suit that had three pieces: a jacket, pants, and a skirt. She could create endless outfits by pairing a different blouse or sweater with the suit pieces, or sometimes by adding a scarf to be a focal point of the outfit. She always looked fashionable and put together. And I truly didn't notice for months that the base was the same.

We went shopping together once and she shared her philosophy—she looked for "investment pieces" rather than the latest fashion. She spent more on a single, beautifully made cashmere sweater than I spent on a season's worth of new items. And then wore it for years. I was thinking in terms of cute individual outfits; she was thinking in terms of versatility and quality. That day she guided me to a sheer black polka-dotted button-up blouse, saying, "That's a great investment piece that will feel modern for a long time." I wore that blouse for ten years. In short, you need a lot less than you think to be functional and fashionable.

Can I Rent or Borrow It?

To believe I need to actually own an item of clothing, I have to convince myself that I will use the item at least semi-frequently for months or even years. If I can't say yes to that statement, then I start to explore whether I can borrow or rent it instead. This is especially useful for special occasions.

When I say borrow, I recognize that your siblings or friends may have different taste, may live in another city, or of course be a different size. If you're lucky enough to have a clothing swap buddy, that's great. My daughter and her friends have traded homecoming dresses, and I wore a fancy lilac dress to my sister's wedding that I borrowed from a friend. Luckily, there are some options to "borrow" from strangers, especially for special occasion outfits that you might use only once. (As a side note, men have rented rather than purchased tuxedos for years; it is only women who have always been expected to purchase expensive, high-fashion items for special events.)

Rent the Runway is a service that lets you browse their inventory online and then ship the outfits of your choice to you in two sizes (to make sure you get the right fit) for five days. Wear it to your event, and then drop it in the prepaid return mailer and it's back out of your closet. It's a lot cheaper than buying new for every occasion, and it keeps you from owning clothes you'll never wear again. They also have local showrooms in big cities so you can actually try it on, take it with you, and return it after wearing.

Le Tote is a wardrobe subscription service that allows you to borrow five items at a time from its inventory—three pieces of clothing and two accessories. Need a cocktail dress? Or a great jacket for that presentation day? Swap out your choices as often as you wish.

If I Can't Borrow It, Can I Get It Gently Used?

Once you wrap your brain around the idea of wearing gently used clothing, there are a ton of sources out there. There are homegrown options like garage sales, charity thrift stores, or eBay, which are pretty time-intensive and a little like Forrest Gump and his box of chocolates—you never know what you're going to get (and you should definitely wash it when you get it). If this is a hobby for you and you enjoy the hunt, that's great. There are online communities like Poshmark, Vinted, Mercari, or Grailed (for men!) where you can buy and often sell used items, which is a great way to keep quality clothing in circulation.

More time-constrained folks can find curated clothing at consignment shops (which are more likely to have high-end items since the price has to allow for the store to get a cut and still be worth the effort for the seller). Or there are also noncharitable thrift and resale stores that have a more discerning eye for inventory and know what is likely to be popular because their business success depends on it.

One of the most progressive companies I've seen in terms of promoting reuse of their own clothing is Patagonia—which has promoted its Threads program as an alternative to buying new. Other retailers joining in the "circular economy" with online resale sites include Lululemon, Eileen Fisher, Levi's, REI, and more. The next time you need rugged outdoor gear or workout clothes, look for their secondhand stores first.

Can I Get It New from an Ethically Produced, Sustainable Source?

If you can't borrow or find a gently used version of the item you want to purchase, what then? Let's say you've determined that you do need a new investment piece. Your overcoat has a stain that won't come out. Or your jeans don't fit now that you've had kids. Maybe you considered a few used options but didn't see anything you liked.

This is the time to search for organic materials and fair labor practices. The good news is that manufacturers who use organic materials and fair labor practices usually produce a high-quality product that is hopefully investment-grade clothing. Some popular brands that pass the mark on their practices include the same ones that sell secondhand (no surprise there), like Levi's, Patagonia, and Eileen Fisher. Other brands that are respected for their overall sustainability and business practices include Everlane, Boden, Cuyana, Indigenous, and Athleta. But there are many tiny, responsible clothing brands probably in your own community. So consider picking up interesting and unique pieces at local boutiques, where you can ask the shopkeeper about the designer and their practices.

Those who value animal rights probably want to avoid leather, suede, snakeskin or crocodile skin, fur, and calf hair. Luckily, many designers are eschewing these materials for faux versions that don't involve animals; somebody is even experimenting with leather made from mushrooms.[7] Vegans might add cashmere, wool, and silk to the "avoid" list.

In any case, I encourage you to pass up fast fashion if your budget allows. If you move to owning fewer higher-quality pieces, you will save money over time, as your wardrobe lasts longer, and you can add a few carefully selected pieces every year.

Can I Get a High-Quality Product That Will Last?

You've done all you could to avoid making frivolous clothing purchases, know you need something specific, and can't borrow it or purchase it from an ethical source. What's left? Buy something that lasts.

I was in Frisco, Colorado, a little mountain town about an hour from where I live in Denver, and we stopped in a shop on the main street after breakfast one morning as we explored the area. This was a unique store filled with fairly expensive clothes (average price of an item was probably $100 or so). The designers were local, the owners were local, and the clothes were "investment grade" materials and construction. I bought a light blue V-neck cashmere sweater—an investment that supported several small businesses in that community. It's simple enough to stay fashionable for years, and it looks and feels lux and beautifully made, so I'm happy to wear it frequently. (If you visit my website or social media, you'll undoubtedly spot that light blue V-neck sweater!)

Purchasing high-quality clothing that is made to last will always be better than purchasing flimsy, disposable items at a fast fashion outlet.

Caring for Your Clothing

Once you own that clothing, be conscious in your care for it.

According to Levi Strauss, about 50 percent of the energy use for their jeans comes from the growing and manufacturing process, and 50 percent comes from our "maintenance" after we purchase them (namely, all that washing and drying).[8] They encourage their customers to wear their jeans multiple times before washing (in cold water!) and consider line-drying to save energy. I find this advice a little harder to follow as a woman who doesn't like the saggy stretch that happens after a few times wearing jeans, but in general I wear work clothes, jeans, and sweaters multiple times before washing or getting them dry-cleaned.

Dry cleaning can itself be an environmentally destructive process. If you have dry-clean-only items, find a "green" cleaner who will use biodegradable chemicals, and ask them *not* to put your clothes in plastic. Now that my kids are in their teens, I find my clothes can make the trip to my car and into my house without getting spilled on and so have started asking for them to hold off on the plastic.

By the way, supporting a small, local dry-cleaning business (rather than a chain) is a great way to "shop local" and support small businesses in your community!

We Are What We Wear

There's an old saying that "we are what we eat." That's true, but also applies to what we wear. Clothing says a lot about who you are. It proclaims your personal style, of course, but also your personal sense of responsibility for others and for our shared world. Putting some thought into what you wear, where it comes from, how you care for it, and what happens to it afterward is a daily part of living an integrated life.

CHAPTER 10

Cleaning: Keeping You and Your Home Clean Naturally

Ironically, one area in which we are in danger of making the environment dirtier is the products we use to keep our bodies and our homes clean. As with food products, a key issue revolves around ingredients and practices that are harmful to the environment, whether in the production process, packaging, chemical contaminants, or creation of trash. Here are some lessons I've learned about minimizing my household's impact while still maintaining a clean home and clean people.

Household Cleaning

Americans can be obsessed with cleaning and germs, but I never have been. One perspective that was influential to me was from a woman who believed strongly that letting kids play in the dirt helped their system learn to deal with and overcome the many little infections, viruses, and bugs (literal and medicinal) that they were exposed to. According to WebMD, "This line of thinking, called the 'hygiene hypothesis,' holds that when exposure to parasites, bacteria, and viruses is *limited* early in life, children face a greater chance of having allergies, asthma, and other autoimmune diseases during adulthood."[1]

But there's a difference between letting your kids play in the mud occasionally, and letting mud and mold run through your house. Our floors, our bathrooms, our refrigerators and dishes, our clothes and carpets and ducts all need to be cleaned regularly. So, even we "free range" parents need to clean, and that usually means cleaning products. Or does it? Can we develop a cleaning hierarchy to match our buying hierarchy?

One basic problem with cleaning is the use of toxic chemicals. We are sold toxic chemicals in spray or aerosol bottles (many of which are not recyclable) for many different uses. If you read the warnings on these bottles, you know how dangerous many of them can be to our health and to the environment, and heaven forbid our kids get ahold of them. Here's the fine print from the can of oven cleaner under my sink:

DANGER: CORROSIVE. CONTAINS SODIUM
HYDROXIDE (LYE). WILL BURN EYES AND

SKIN. HARMFUL IF SWALLOWED. Avoid contact with eyes, skin, mucous membranes and clothing. DO NOT ingest. Use only with adequate ventilation. Avoid breathing spray mist. Wear long rubber gloves when using.

Uh-huh. Sounds pretty harmful to humans. Imagine that getting washed down your pipes and into the water supply. What does it do to the water quality, and the wildlife that drink or live in those waters? Now how many other chemical cleaners have similar warnings and also end up in our water supply?

New Mexico State University points out, "Often, retail household cleaning products contain substances that are deemed hazardous. It is difficult to identify these substances because manufacturers are allowed to label these substances as confidential business information (CBI). The U.S. Environmental Protection Agency (EPA) has acknowledged that the inappropriate and excessive use of CBI claims has hidden important information from the public and even from EPA offices."[2]

Ultimately, my objective in cleaning is to reach my family's personal standard of "clean" using the fewest toxic chemicals along the way. If you agree with that objective, consider the following cleaning hierarchy that mimics the purchasing hierarchy described previously.

DOES IT NEED TO BE CLEANED NOW?

The first step is to consider whether it needs to be cleaned yet. Everyone has different tolerance levels with cleanliness: I follow a guy on Twitter who washes his bath towels after every single use—this seems like an unhealthy obsession to me, but my own timeline of weekly or semiweekly washes seems gross to him. (I mean, you're clean when you use a towel; how dirty could it get?)

So for some things, evaluate how often you need to clean the item or location. Can you wear that sweater again before washing or dry cleaning? Can you wait and fill the last few spots on the bottom rack before running the dishwasher? Can you combine laundry from multiple family members to get a full load before running the machine?

Getting the most out of each cleaning will make the resources you do use go further and reduce the overall amount of cleaner you use.

USE WATER + PATIENCE AS MUCH AS POSSIBLE

Another way to reduce chemicals: patience. One trick I've noticed, in the kitchen especially, is that the magic formula for cleaning stoves and counters is simple: water + time. If I use a sponge to pool some water on a blob of marinara and then continue putting dishes in the dishwasher, I can come back in three minutes or so and the food is loosened enough to wipe with the sponge, no chemicals necessary. For daily wipe downs, clean water might be enough.

TRY NATURAL PRODUCTS IF YOU NEED SOMETHING STRONGER

When you do need to clean something, and water won't do the trick, the next best step is a natural cleaner like distilled white vinegar. Advocates of vinegar suggest you can use it for almost anything—cleaning tubs and showers and counters and floors and even clothes. Search Pinterest for "use vinegar for cleaning" and you'll find simple recipes and ratios for dozens of cleaning applications. Here are a few examples of how we use it:

- Mix equal parts vinegar and water and spray in your refrigerator to remove odors, avoid mold and mildew, or remove any that have cropped up. Or clean and degrease the kitchen cabinets (especially those that are near the stovetop).

- Mix vinegar with baking soda and hydrogen peroxide to create a cleaner for your bathroom.

- A fine spray bottle of vinegar or vinegar and water can deodorize and freshen carpets, draperies, upholstery, and other fabrics; that same spray can be used around entryways to repel bugs and spiders.

- Mix vinegar with baking soda to create a paste that you can use to clean your oven, your carpet, stained ceramic, and more.

- Microwave a mixture of vinegar and water for five minutes to create steam and then wipe the sides of the microwave down. Everything will be soft and easy to remove.

- Run diluted vinegar through your coffee maker to clean it, followed by several rounds of plain water. I promise it won't leave a weird smell or taste in your coffee.

- Use the old-school volcano to freshen or unclog a drain: sprinkle baking soda followed by vinegar.

- Equal parts vinegar and hydrogen peroxide make a great paste to clean and deodorize cutting boards. I also use lemon halves after I have squeezed them for something else—rub the cut side on the board before applying the paste.

- Use vinegar in place of fabric softener in the laundry—it is especially useful for towels and other items that can get damp and musty. (If your towels or workout clothes smell musty when you use them, even right after you washed them, this is the solution.)

BUY GREEN CLEANING PRODUCTS

Sometimes vinegar concoctions won't cut it, despite what the Pinterest enthusiasts want to tell you. So if you need something stronger to get that stain or smell out, search for green cleaners, as certified by an independent organization like Green Seal, the EPA's "Safer Choice" program, or an ECOLOGO label. If you can't find the seal, seek out words like "nontoxic," "biodegradable," and "hypoallergenic."

In addition to what's in the bottle, pay attention to the bottle itself. Glass is the most recyclable, and more companies are offering refillable bottles, whether glass or plastic. Then you just have to purchase the refill pods and add water to keep using the same spray bottle over and over.

Another important new development in green cleaning (and beverages and other products) is the commitment by companies to reduce or eliminate their use of "virgin" plastic in favor of post-consumer recycled plastic. You can support this transition by purchasing cleaners in bottles that are not only recycl*able* but themselves the product of a recycling effort.

Personal Care

In addition to keeping your household clean, most of us like to keep ourselves clean and deodorized, and it's amazing how many chemicals go into what seems like a simple idea. If you've lived in another culture with different standards or values around cleanliness, you may realize that Americans are unusually obsessed with body odor and will go to great lengths to mask or avoid it. (Americans except, apparently, Ashton Kutcher and Mila Kunis.)

I can't help but think about all the chemicals we willingly apply to the largest organ in our body—our skin—every day. According to the Environmental Working Group, "On average, women use 12 personal care products a day, exposing themselves to 168 chemical ingredients. Men use six, exposing themselves to 85 unique chemicals."[3] For consumers in the United States, the vast majority of those chemicals have not been thoroughly tested for consumer safety, thanks to a complicated and outdated regulatory framework. Some of them are known to be toxic, to disrupt hormones, and even our reproductive system. According to *The Guardian*, "In cosmetics alone, the EU has banned or restricted more than 1,300 chemicals while the US has outlawed or curbed just 11."[4]

You might think, *What's the harm in a tiny little bit that's in my deodorant?* Probably there wouldn't be any harm, if it were in fact a tiny little bit. But when you apply that chemical to yourself every single day over a lifetime, it adds up. Thinking about the impact of applying small amounts of daily chemicals on myself kinda made me shrug, but when my kids got old enough to start using deodorant and other personal products, suddenly the thought of starting them down this path to a lifetime of accumulated chemical load and the associated health impacts was unacceptable. So I started researching topics like aluminum-free deodorant and ingredients to avoid in shampoo.

That's when I learned that the potential danger of these chemicals isn't just to you and your health but to the environment, too: "When we use personal care products, we don't tend to acknowledge how they will end up in the environment. When your shampoo washes down the drain, when you swim in the ocean with sunscreen on, or when you throw out a bottle with a little bit of product left, it all will likely end up in rivers, oceans, and lakes. This harms animal and plant life in marine ecosystems and continues through the food chain."[5]

In addition to the chemicals they contain, all those little plastic bottles end up in landfills if we aren't careful about buying recyclable packaging or reusing items.

THE PERSONAL CLEANING HIERARCHY

Similar to our household cleaning, we might first ask if we can reduce the amount of cleaning we do—I'm not suggesting that you don't brush your teeth twice a day (definitely do, and floss, too), but if your hair doesn't feel oily, you probably don't need to wash it every day (ask your hairstylist). By reducing the frequency, you automatically put fewer chemicals on your body and into the environment.

In addition to reducing the use of any given product, you might commit to not buying so many in the first place. If you think of each perfume, each body wash, and each eye shadow as having an environmental impact in its production, use, and disposal, do you really need that seventh shade? Since most women, myself included, don't usually use up all of a cosmetic product (like lipsticks or eye shadows), you might commit to using up one product before buying another as a way to limit your purchasing.

Much like vinegar for household cleaning, an amazing natural product that serves as an all-around personal cleaner is *coconut oil.* Several years ago I started buying jars of coconut oil and keep finding new uses for it. Again, if you do an online search, you'll come up with dozens of ideas; here are a few of my favorites:

- Coconut oil removes makeup, including mascara. I wash my face at night by just putting a dime-size blob of coconut oil on my fingers and rubbing it into my face before wiping with a steamy washcloth. No other cleanser necessary.

- Coconut oil has antibacterial properties, so I dab it on healing cuts and scrapes, and my cuticles after I've removed a hangnail.

- We use it for after-sun skin care, especially on the kids' faces where even aloe might get in their eyes and burn (coconut oil won't burn).

- You can create face masks and body scrubs with coconut oil as the base, using sugar, honey, essential oils, or other add-ins.

- Coconut oil melts with the warmth of your hands, so it can be a great base for massage oils for you or your little ones.

- Coconut oil makes a great shaving aid or aftershave lotion.

- Some people also use it as a hair mask or (in small amounts) a leave-in conditioner or to help tame frizzy hair.

Personally, I use the Dr. Bronner's pure castile soap as my body wash and shaving lather. It receives an "A" rating from the Environmental Working Group[6] and can be used for personal care or a great deal of other cleaning—including laundry, all-purpose cleaning, hand washing, and more. It's even safe enough for babies, though I would avoid the eucalyptus or peppermint varieties, as the zing of these essential oils in the soap might be too strong for young ones. The Environmental Working Group site (https://www.ewg.org/guides/cleaners) lets you check out how your current cleaner stacks up and, if necessary, find a greener alternative.

Staying Clean without Making the World Dirtier

As with all areas of an integrated life, most of us can start taking smaller steps in the right direction even if we're not ready to go all in.

For example, if household cleaning is an area you'd like to tackle, consider some steps that might help you move in the right direction even if you don't give up traditional cleaners entirely:

- Try using one of the vinegar solutions listed above for three weeks of the month and then a heavier industrial cleaner the fourth week.

- Stretch out the time between deep cleanings so that you might use fewer chemicals over the course of a year.

- Switch out your conventional cleaner for a greener one.

- Use cleaners that are available in refillable bottles to reduce the environmental impact of the packaging.

If you want to go further, find a "zero waste" provider that allows you to bring in your refillable (preferably glass) containers and pay by weight: shampoo, laundry detergent, body wash, and more. The same store may stock many other helpful items for reducing your waste and chemical load: washcloths and reusable cotton rounds, natural sponges, and the like. We try to avoid disposable wipes, dusting cloths, and the like in favor of microfiber cloths. They can be washed and reused over and over. We also have a set of reusable cloths to replace paper towels and disposable napkins. All these cleaning cloths go into a bin with kitchen towels, and when the bin is full, they get washed (with vinegar!) and then reused.

To simplify your search for products that are healthy for you and the environment, you might consult MightyNest (https://mightynest.com), which carefully screens the ingredients of every product they sell to only include ones that are good for you, and good for the environment. They'll also help you swap out your plastic containers and disposables with bamboo, glass, stainless steel, and cloth alternatives, one step at a time.

CHAPTER 11

Money: Wielding Your Financial Power for Shared Prosperity

My professional journey in philanthropy took a significant turn when I (and many others) started asking questions—not about where our employers were giving grants but where they were making and investing the money that funded our grantmaking budget. Foundations must give away about 5 percent of their assets each year in the form of grants (and expenses that support the grantmaking). But what was happening with the other 95 percent of the funds? What was that money doing, and was it aligned with the charitable purpose of the foundation? After all, it's nineteen times more money than the grants! To put that into dollars, a foundation with a $1 billion endowment gives away about $50 million in grants, while the other $950 million is sitting in investments. Which pool of money, do you think, is having a bigger impact?

When philanthropists across the field started looking deeper, many found the answers to these questions unsettling. Most foundations had enacted a firewall between their grantmaking and their investing, believing they had to make as much money as possible, however they could, because a larger endowment meant a larger grantmaking budget. Some argued that to even consider nonfinancial factors (like social impact) was a dereliction of their fiduciary duty to the foundation. That seemed patently ridiculous to me. Wouldn't it be better to have *all* the money working toward your social mission? Wasn't your duty to the mission of the foundation, not to growing its bank balance? Many others raised these issues, and the field of "impact investing" was born.

And yet it took me years to apply this same scrutiny to my own financial situation. I always thought I didn't have enough money to make a difference. I didn't have millions like a foundation, so I needed to maximize return for my retirement. I am just one little consumer; I couldn't make the financial system work with my values at my tiny level of economic activity. Eventually, I realized that when you add up my everyday transactions like grocery shopping, bill paying, paying for insurance and a mortgage, using credit cards, and building a small emergency fund, I moved tens of thousands of dollars through the financial system every year—and that money could be having an impact along the way.

Even if you don't have a lot of money for discretionary spending, you probably interact with the financial system nearly every day. Hopefully you have a checking and savings account, maybe a credit card or several, a mortgage or a car loan, and perhaps some investments, either through a work-based 401(k) or, if you're really doing well, in an after-tax brokerage account. Even when you're not using it, your money can be working in alignment with your values—or not.

Banking: What to Know about Where You Keep Your Money

We are in an ultra-low interest rate environment right now, so you probably aren't earning much on whatever money you have sitting in a checking or savings account. But what *is* happening to your money when it's sitting in a bank, either in a savings account, money market, CDs, or in other products? The answer is that it's being lent out.

- Depositors (like you) provide funds that the bank can lend out.

- The bank lends it out and charges interest to the borrower.

- The bank gives some of those earnings back to the person who provided the funds in the first place, giving them an incentive to keep the deposits with them.

Even now, banks pay you something like 0.25 percent annual interest; where do they get that money? They lend it to someone else at something like 4 percent, cover their expenses, keep a profit, and give you a tiny sliver as a thank-you for letting them use your money. Your savings account is funding their loan business.

Is that necessarily bad? No. But there is a vast difference between *to whom* and *how* different banks lend the money they have available to them. Traditional banks lend it to corporations, to well-established businesses with positive cash flow, and to households with higher credit scores. Many also lend to oil pipeline projects and other fossil fuel developments, to the tune of more than $3.8 trillion in the last five years since the Paris Climate Accords.[1] Such borrower profiles are safer for them to make sure they get their money back (plus interest income). They also have shareholders clamoring for higher profits every year, so many extract as much as they can in fees (ATM fees, deposit fees, overdraft fees, annual fees, inactivity fees, statement fees, and on and on). The three largest banks in 2015 (Wells Fargo, Bank of America, and Chase) each made around $5 billion in fee income that year, more than three times the fee income of the fifth largest, U.S. Bank.[2]

More recently, you may have seen the ongoing scandals involving Wells Fargo and how they accumulated all that fee income. Turns out, they pushed so hard to expand their business that associates opened millions of fake accounts, charged inappropriate mortgage fees, applied unneeded auto insurance, and initiated other fee-producing activities without the consent of their customers.[3] When the customers saw those unexpected fees on their statements (and up to twenty thousand people had their vehicles repossessed!), the world discovered the company-wide fraud. As a result, Wells Fargo has paid more than $2 billion so far in customer refunds and regulatory fines.[4] Newly installed executives have blamed an "out of control" sales culture and fired 5,300 employees, promising to turn things around. But that culture was created by the pressure to generate fee income and pad the bank's quarterly profits, which in turn increased the stock price, generating wealth for those who own stock—namely, their shareholders and executives.

Of course, not all big banks promote or tolerate the kind of widespread fraud seen at Wells Fargo, to be sure. They are just "normal" businesses who put the interests of their shareholders first, which can still mean they are chasing short-term quarterly profits to keep the stock price trending upward. To be fair, thanks to the Community Reinvestment Act of 1977 (CRA), banks must designate a portion of their funding to "help meet the credit needs of the communities in which they do business, including low- and moderate-income (LMI) neighborhoods."[5] This leads them to engage in lending around affordable housing, community services, and economic development efforts, often by partnering with local community development financial institutions (CDFIs). Overall, the CRA is generally regarded as preventing the kind of ongoing redlining that occurred in the decades before it was enacted—when banks discriminated against low-income (often minority) neighborhoods and wouldn't offer mortgages or other services there.

But traditional banks aren't the only option for financial services. There are other financial institutions that promote shared prosperity, an approach also known as stakeholder capitalism, which seeks to balance the interests of owners (shareholders) with those of other people who have an interest in how the business is run, including employees, customers, vendors, and the larger community. One important example is *credit unions*. A credit union is owned by its members, the people who use its services. And while it is managed by professionals who make decisions about fees, rates charged to borrowers, and interest rates paid to savers, the focus is on the members and what's best for them. Maintaining a financially healthy business is obviously part of the equation, but extracting maximum value from the customers in favor of the credit union is not. You can also find small or medium-sized regional banks that are more focused on investing locally and with the financial health of the region in mind.

So to the extent you are able, *putting your resources into a community-based credit union or community-minded bank will have more positive financial ripple effects throughout your community.* I'm not going to lie, though: such a change requires you to *resist the allure of convenience* and put shared prosperity at the top of your priorities. It took me years to make this switch myself.

I had belonged to a local credit union when I lived in Philadelphia many years ago but closed the account when I moved away. Back in the early 2000s, the big disadvantage to credit unions was the lack of ATMs, since we all spent mostly cash and made deposits (direct deposit wasn't a thing back then) at an actual bank branch. My new employer was in a different state and I was traveling for work and to visit family, so finding an institution with a big, national network of ATMs made sense, and I opened my new accounts at a big, national bank. Over the following years, I moved through three more states; the big, national bank was there in all of them, with plenty of ATMs. The bank was pretty early to offer a solid online banking website and mobile app that were much more developed than those available from smaller, localized credit unions. Super convenient. So what made me finally switch?

In 2020 my husband and I decided to buy a used car (all my cars are used!), and at the dealership we got offered a lousy rate—they said it was the age of the car that was the influencing factor. I thought it might be time to make the move to a local credit union to get a friendlier auto loan and used that little push to start the process of opening accounts at a local credit union.

At first, it was definitely not convenient. I had to go into the branch four or five times—the actual, physical bank branch (horrors)! I had to call customer service and email them, and they would email me back a day later with an answer. Not terrible, I know, but also not quite the efficient (and person-free) experience I had enjoyed with my big, national bank. And the real kicker was that, in the end, their rate for the car loan was no better than the commercial bank—because of the age of the vehicle.

But I am still glad I did it. After that initial onboarding, the experience has been largely the same, and I can get what I need from the website and mobile app. But instead of funding loans to major corporations and environmentally destructive business practices, I am funding my own community. My money is helping my neighbors to buy a car, buy a house, expand their business, and more, at better interest rates. Access to capital is such a fundamental building block to a more just society. I want my funds to contribute to the world I want to see. (And I am making a better interest rate on my savings to boot.)

If you're not ready yet to make a big switch on your checking or savings, consider researching the rates at a local credit union or regional bank the next time you need a car or home loan. You can also seek out a bank that aligns with your values through the Global Alliance for Banking on Values (https://www.gabv.org), "a network of independent banks using finance to deliver sustainable economic, social and environmental development." They have fourteen member institutions (including credit unions) in the US and Canada, and forty-plus more around the world. Many have online services and belong to a network of ATMs, so you can live anywhere and still be a customer.

Credit Cards

I rarely carry physical money anymore. I barely use my checkbook. Instead, most of my transactions are virtual, 1s and 0s moving from a credit card terminal or over an internet connection. I have six plastic cards in my wallet right now that I use to do most of my transacting, including three store-specific cards, a debit card, and a few different general-purpose credit cards. One of them gives me 1.5 percent cash back on all my purchases, and for years I have redeemed that cash back for gift cards for nonessentials like Starbucks (for me) and Barnes and Noble (a favorite gift for teachers, young kids, and anyone who loves to learn).

How does the credit card manage to pay me 1.5 percent cash back? Because, like banks paying you interest on your savings account, credit cards charge the merchants more than that, keep some for their efforts, and return a slice to you as a thank-you. Businesses that accept credit cards pay between 1.5 and 3.5 percent on each purchase as a fee to the service providers that make it super easy to get the funds out of your account and deposit it into theirs.

What if the credit card issuer got creative with how their fees were used and spent them in a way that promoted shared prosperity? There are more socially minded credit card issuers popping up all the time. Check out Amalgamated Bank, Aspiration, and Southern Bancorp (also a member of GABV) for some options that use your credit card transactions to plant trees, donate to charities, support minority-owned businesses, and otherwise integrate your values with your money. It literally costs you nothing.

Becoming a Responsible Investor

I was lucky enough to start my professional career at a place that offered a 401(k) that I could contribute to, and they even matched some of my contributions! The organization once offered a class to help educate the staff about the importance of saving for retirement. They gave us a calculator, and when I put in my variables—age, current salary, expected retirement age, and an annual rate of return—if I used 7 percent as the annual rate of return, the calculator said I would have $7 million by the time I retired! I was ecstatic!

Now, let's say I am halfway to retirement and not anywhere close to halfway to that goal. As I prepared to leave the steady paycheck and benefits of an organization to pursue an integrated life as both a consultant and author, my husband and I saved as much as we could in emergency funds. And finally decided to get an investment advisor.

We found a match in a financial advisor who is helping us to develop a life plan and invest in line with our values. We've collected up the various retirement accounts from all over the country into IRAs for each of us, and were able to shift some of our emergency funds into an investment account. Since the amounts are still pretty modest ("modest" by investment standards, I acknowledge that just having an investment portfolio puts me in the top 1 percent of global wealth), the accounts are invested in a diverse mix of mutual funds.

FINDING RESPONSIBLE MUTUAL FUNDS

What's new and exciting to me is that all of my ten mutual funds are what's known as *ESG screened*. ESG stands for Environmental, Social, and Governance. An ESG fund is one that defines specific criteria for what it will consider a socially responsible company— these definitions vary from fund to fund—then screens individual companies against those metrics. The mutual fund provider will then group the stocks of individual companies that meet their criteria into a mutual fund, and market it to potential investors.

Two important details to know are that different mutual funds focus on different aspects of the E, the S, and the G, and that there is no single definition that is agreed on by everyone. Therefore, you can't assume that any given fund marketed as ESG is going to be a good choice for you. For example, two funds might interpret "social" behaviors quite differently:

- The YWCA has a fund (ticker symbol WOMN) that screens for companies that enact policies favorable to the well-being and promotion of women, like paid family leave, the number of women executives or board members, and other family-friendly benefits. They promote the adoption of women-friendly business practices by providing a "carrot" of inclusion in their fund, and they also use the fees earned from this fund to support the YWCA, providing an innovative, sustainable revenue stream.

- McDonald's scores well on these social measures and is a star in their particular fund. But of course, another fund might be screening on how a company contributes to health in society, and McDonald's would not make the cut.

The majority of us (those with investable assets under $5 million) are most likely to be invested in mutual funds and stocks that are publicly traded. Millions of shares change hands every day, and the price of a company's shares is largely dictated by the earnings and potential future earnings of the company, not by its social responsibility. With each company having hundreds of millions, billions, or even trillions of dollars of stock owned in the market, our individually tiny bit of money—whether we personally own a particular stock or not—is not going to move that stock's price. But when we work together as a massive social movement, we can force companies to take socially responsible actions. The movement toward ESG-positive stocks is gaining momentum and has the potential to bring about this kind of change—if we can avoid the "greenwashing" and "causewashing" that tries to make companies look good while going about their business as usual—and make sure the underlying actions are positive.

Perhaps the most famous example of massive buying and selling of stocks in the public market leading to change is the campaign to disinvest in South Africa during apartheid: "The global boycott against South Africa's apartheid regime was the largest of its kind in the second half of the 20th century. This divestment movement is credited, in part, for helping to end the systemically racist, white-ruled government in 1994."[6] That successful effort has been an inspiration to the modern ESG and more specific issue-driven movements.

Today, the big push in public stocks is to take your money out of companies that deal in fossil fuels. This selling of a particular stock or an entire industry is called "disinvesting." In 2014, the Rockefeller Brothers Fund announced that they were disinvesting their endowment from fossil fuels.[7] They weren't the first to do so, but given how the Rockefeller fortune was created, this move caused quite a stir.

Critics said, "That's great, but it's just 'virtue signaling' and will have no impact whatsoever on the companies and how they do business." And my colleagues inside the effort said, "You're right— it *is* virtue signaling. And we hope others will see this signal and make moves of their own in line with their values." Rockefeller Brothers Fund was right—many others have, including universities, other foundation endowments, and plenty of ESG funds now screen out fossil fuel companies and those who support them. Students often lead the charge and have found success in securing disinvestment commitments at prestigious educational institutions like Yale, Columbia University, Oxford, Cambridge, Brown University, Georgetown, University of Michigan, and the University of California system.[8] In September of 2021, holdout Harvard University finally joined in the disinvestment movement, after years of student and faculty advocacy, saying, "Climate change is the most consequential threat facing humanity."[9]

The collection of public commitments does add up. As more and more voices join the chorus and make public statements and disinvest, this puts pressure on a company's stock price and also makes it more expensive for them to borrow money. Those are real disincentives for them to continue the behavior.

Think Long Term

I've always told the investment committees I work with that ESG investing is about having a long-term outlook. The same is true for you and me: if you are not currently in retirement or expect to be there in the next five years or so, skate to where the puck is going, not where it is now—that is, think about what you want and expect the world to look like in ten or twenty years and invest accordingly. Fossil fuels are on their way out, so why wait until we wring the last drop of quarterly value and the share prices start dropping? Why not just move your money to where the future is? Especially in environmental issues—electric vehicles, clean energy, water management, ocean cleanup, and alternatives to meat and plastic—these are the growth industries of the next century.

If you have additional assets that are invested for growth, there is much you can do across a diversified portfolio in many different asset classes, from green bonds to impact-themed venture funds, to Opportunity Zone real estate investments. Many of these investments allow you to earn a return while helping neighbors who want to own a home, small businesses trying to create jobs, and governments looking to build green infrastructure.

First, find a financial advisor who specializes in *impact investing*—not one who says, "Sure, we have those ESG funds on our platform"—because there is much more to impact investing for those with more significant assets. Second, be sure to ask your advisor about first-time fund managers and those from underrepresented groups, including women, racial minorities, and LGBTQ+ communities. Those managers often see new markets and new opportunities because of their life experiences and can help your portfolio take advantage of tomorrow's big market opportunities that have been historically ignored.

Viewing all your financial transactions together, you are probably moving tens of thousands of dollars through the financial system every year. *Know your power*, and think about how to keep your assets aligned with your purpose, even (and especially!) when you're not using them.

CHAPTER 12

Charity: Using Your Time and Money Wisely

Nonprofits represent 5.6 percent of the economy and employ 12.3 million people.[1] And Americans give more than $1 billion to charities every day;[2] in fact, 73 percent of Americans donate to a charity, and 58 percent volunteer.[3] We are a uniquely charitable people: Americans give more to charity than the citizens of any other country. And yet our giving is not always as thoughtful and impactful as it could be.

Selecting a Charity: Understanding the Difference between Good Causes and Good Programs

Dan Pallotta once wrote a column for *Harvard Business Review* calling on charities to start treating their donors as intelligent adults.[4] It made me want to stand up and cheer. And in rising up to meet his challenge, I am here to tell you a hard truth. That truth is that most of you are doing a terrible job picking charities to receive your hard-earned money and carry the torch of your ideals.

As a person who makes social change her full-time profession, I am often frustrated that big-hearted individuals hear about the mission of a charity and say, "Isn't that a wonderful charity?"

Let me be clear: it is impossible to know whether a charity is good or bad, wasteful or efficient, simply by reading its mission statement. Why do I say this? Primarily because I know that a mission statement is a statement of intentions, not a statement of accomplishments. *A good cause is not the same thing as a good program.* And we all have good intentions, but the inconvenient truth in social change work is that good intentions are not enough.

Consider that in 2010, ten Americans were arrested for attempting to kidnap thirty-three Haitian children after the devastating earthquake there.[5] They were missionaries whose desire to "save" children from post-earthquake Haiti almost resulted in loving parents and their children being permanently separated.

Or the effort by international aid groups to send misprinted Super Bowl champion T-shirts to people in the third world (including Haiti), improving their organization's overhead ratios by claiming the value of these gifts-in-kind as program expenses.

In reality, the goods they were sending are readily available even to poor people in the target geographies, widely accepted by the aid community as having the effect of undermining local businesses and creating a culture of dependency, and otherwise causing harm to the very communities they were purporting to help.[6]

Or consider a "battered mothers resource fund" that never actually implemented any programs it was fundraising for and potentially scared women away from seeking help by falsely claiming that many shelters separate mothers from their children.[7] I bet those supporters read the mission statement and said, "That's a worthy cause."

You know, they're right: it *is* a worthy cause. But it's not a worthwhile program. This idea that different women's shelters are implementing radically different programs, some of which might be harmful to women, is something we don't often consider. But the same concern is necessary for all kinds of charities.

Some jobs programs help people spiff up their resumes and place them in dead end jobs. Others provide holistic training to prepare them for a lifetime of success in a new career. Sadly, some don't even know what results they're getting because they are too busy playing with allocation of costs to make their overhead ratio as low as possible. Some animal shelters euthanize animals; some don't. Some "social service" agencies refuse to serve people in need because of their gender identity or sexual orientation; others serve everyone.

As a person with good intentions, what can you do? You can pick an issue and learn about it. In fact, I insist on it. Don't give to any organization that asks just because it's a good cause. Don't give, thinking, *What's the harm? What's the worst that could happen?*

If you know nothing about that cause, that issue, that organization, you *can* be actually doing harm, as the examples here illustrate. Withholding your donation when you don't know what you're doing is as important a moral act as giving when asked.

The father of a childhood friend of mine used to say, "Don't be so open-minded that your brains fall out."

THE LIMITATIONS OF OVERHEAD RATIOS

These days, it's become popular for people to use Charity Navigator and similar online sites to get a report card on the charities they want to support. While those services provide some useful information about a charity's level of transparency, be aware that their reports are viewed with extreme skepticism by professionals. That's because an overhead ratio—the percentage of expenses spent on administration versus program expenses—is an extremely flawed metric.

In 2008, Jan Masaoka of Blue Avocado wrote, "When financial metrics are used to compare nonprofits, the results are often destructive. Two nonprofits, each working with children with disabilities, can show hugely different costs for serving the same number of children. When government agencies, foundations, and donors compare financial performance, they may not realize that one is working with upper-income children with dyslexia while the other is working with low-income children with autism."[8] Pressuring the second to improve its financial performance means pressuring it to work with children from higher-income families, and with less severe disabilities.

Masaoka points out that it's almost impossible to compare the financial performance of any two charities even if they work in similar fields—such as counseling centers, environmental groups, and so on—unless you have details about what people they work with, the communities where they are located, their leadership and operational styles, and so on.

Sites like Charity Navigator are not measuring a nonprofit's performance so much as the savvy of its accountant in assigning as many dollars as possible to "program" line items instead of "admin" line items to make the ratio look good. Asking nonprofits to focus on these ratios may be distracting at best and damaging at worst. They don't even purport to measure the effectiveness of the charity at accomplishing actual social results that the charity was formed to accomplish. So please don't ask about a charity's overhead ratio; it has almost nothing to do with effectiveness.

SO WHAT IS A DONOR TO DO?

It's a real problem. You want to be a responsible donor but don't know what you're supposed to be looking at, especially if the most commonly used financial metrics are out. In my experience, you can be better than you think at evaluating charities. Individual donors have some powerful ways to make decisions about charities they are considering donating to.

1. *Give where you live.* Individual donors are, I think, best suited to give locally. They can see the needs in their own community, and they can see the nonprofits at work there. You can follow the local press coverage, hear the locals talk about problems and people working to solve them,

and heck, you *are* a local so your own personal opinion counts, too.

2. *Look for charities that address a real need.* A good sign for this is that they have members of the neighborhood involved in the planning. Outsiders are not nearly as good at designing programs to "help" people as people are at identifying the help they need. Check the board roster. If it's composed solely of bank presidents and big-name lawyers, the nonprofit may be good at fundraising, but you'll need to dig deeper on the question of addressing need.

3. *Follow the leaders.* Many local nonprofits are fairly small shops, and they are highly dependent on the vision and leadership of a founder. That can be good and bad, but it definitely means you need to have confidence in the organization's leader. Chances are you can actually see this leader in action if you are focusing on a local nonprofit. There's a great discussion of how to get the most from visiting charities in the book *Grassroots Philanthropy* by Bill Somerville.

4. *If you really care about financials, research their operating budget.* I'm no accountant, but as a former grant writer for a struggling nonprofit, I learned that it wasn't going to look good if the funder asked for the operating budget. Unlike the balance sheet, the operating budget would show that last year we didn't raise enough money to cover our operations. That is, we were running an operating

deficit. View their published annual reports. If nonprofits are running red for several years in a row, it's a sign that their business model isn't working out. They probably either need to do a major retooling or go out of business.

5. *Get out there and see the programs they put on.* This means that if they are a charity providing after-school mentoring, go see the program in action, or go to get trained as a mentor. Find a way to be around the kids that are supposed to be benefiting and see if they are, in fact, benefiting. (Volunteering is a great, low-risk way to see how the charity is really run and if the programs seem to be effective.)

6. *After all this, trust your instincts.* You're a smart person. You can tell from this whether the organization is well-run, whether they have their act together. You don't need numbers-crunching and star ratings to tell you they are paying too much for pencils. If you think they're making a difference on an important problem, then you should feel good about your donation.

Pros and Cons of Embedded Charity

Besides any charities you deliberately choose to give to, there are many times where you are offered a chance to give at the spur of the moment. For example, if you've ever gone through a checkout line at a retail store, there's a good chance you've been asked to "round up" a purchase price or add a few dollars to an otherwise ordinary purchase to go toward a charity. Or perhaps you use the Amazon Smile program or have an investment fund by which you allocate a (very small) percentage of your fee toward a charity sponsored by the organization. That is *embedded philanthropy*, a term coined by Lucy Bernholz.[9]

The practice sounds harmless, right? But maybe it's not as clear cut as you think.

- Here's what's *potentially good*: it brings charity into our everyday lives and makes it easy. It allows us to express our identity and our values and align our consumer behavior with the causes we care about. I think we have to start using our purchasing power in this way to motivate corporate actors to behave in more socially responsible ways because corporations are some of the most important actors in this chess game of social change.

- Here's what's *potentially bad*: it could make us thoughtless about philanthropy, and it could end up being a corporate whitewashing tactic, by which companies pay a relatively small percentage of profits to convey an image of corporate social responsibility that may not be backed up by the rest of their labor, environmental, and social practices. When corporations cap their donations (that is, they set out a maximum donation amount) regardless of the number of units sold, it's unclear that individual purchases actually increase the amount of money going to charity or if they just burnish the corporate reputation of the advertiser. I think this is a real danger.

So, like most things—everything from marketing to elected offices to butter—embedded philanthropy is a neutral tool that can be used for good or evil. We have to figure out how to use it responsibly so that, as people who are invested in positive social change and real corporate citizenship, we shouldn't just wait and hope for the best.

Charities themselves are on the front lines of this effort. They are the ones that allow their names and images to be used by the drugstores and clothing retailers and the credit card companies. And to be practical, the promise of a steady stream of corporate dollars and the backing of a corporate marketing budget is incredibly enticing.

But charities need to make sure that the corporations who approach them for embedded philanthropy opportunities act in a way that is consistent with the nonprofit's values. Not just talk in that way in a couple of feel-good meetings but act in that way through their everyday business practices. They should ask the same questions they would of any fundraiser or telemarketer who is asking to represent them and their cause to the public.

Personally, I always decline the round-up or "add a dollar for charity" solicitations, and I definitely do not donate to cold callers and street solicitors. Sometimes it feels cold, but saying no to random requests is saying no to unvetted charities and saying yes to my own self-determined charitable organizations.

Where Are You Giving Now?

I hope charitable giving is already a part of your budget, even if only a small part. Maybe you follow a practice of tithing, steadily giving

5 or 10 percent of income to your church. Maybe you give when people do fundraisers on Facebook or GoFundMe. Maybe you read about an organization in the newspaper that seems like a good cause. Maybe you or your family really benefited from the work of a particular charity and you support them to "pay it forward."

There are many reasons and circumstances that spur charitable donations. But rarely do we think purposefully about our giving as a whole and whether it is living up to our intentions. I learned many lessons about this subject, advising families on how to use their money for social good.

For example, one family was incredibly generous with charitable donations, having made hundreds of millions of dollars when they sold the company they had built over thirty years. But they weren't terribly satisfied with what their donations had accomplished. They felt scattered and like the donations didn't add up to anything beyond a couple of cool projects along the way. One of the first things I did with them was review their history of giving over the last ten years and classify all the previous gifts they had made against the causes they wanted to support—their religious community, education, and treatment for diabetes (which affected a member of the founding generation).

When I went to classify their gifts according to these causes, I found a few details that I shared with the family, much to their surprise:

- I couldn't classify something like 40 percent of the gifts they had made under any of their identified causes; the choices seemed random.

- They had rarely given to the same organization more than once, or for more than a few years, other than their own parish.

When I asked them to explain how they came to make the donations I couldn't classify, they were quick to remember each one: "Jenny whose family sits two pews over from us in church asked me to support her marathon fundraiser for that cause she is passionate about" or "My colleague Paul is on the board of that organization and asked me to contribute" or "Our neighbors invited us to attend that gala with them."

Taken individually, these contributions were relatively small, and each had a relationship attached to them. But taken together, they siphoned significant resources away from the family's intended impact. There were family members who really valued this kind of philanthropy as supporting community causes, and others who thought it was more socializing than anything else and wanted to eliminate it.

After talking it through, the family members struck a balance. In addition to the three main areas they supported, they designated a bucket of giving as the "pew fund" (referring to the folks making requests based on social or religious bonds—those who sat two pews over every week in church). And they limited the pew fund to no more than 15 percent of their annual giving budget. In practice, this meant setting a cap on the size of individual donations in response to ad hoc requests. Some would be smaller than they had been historically. But they agreed to make their named priorities actual budgetary priorities (after all, what is a budget but a statement of our priorities?).

Additionally, we talked about why they didn't keep giving to the same organizations each year. Did they not think they were well-managed organizations or not doing good work? Did the organizations do something to lose their trust? No, they said, it was just that they felt like they should spread their money around to many people, and they also felt kind of bored by giving money to the same people all the time; they wanted to be more "innovative." Other members worried that the organizations would become dependent on their donations and fail to seek new donors or take them for granted.

As someone who has worked with hundreds of individuals and families, I have seen versions of these concerns raised many times even if they aren't expressed quite in this way. This thinking is well-intentioned but ultimately not helpful: being a consistent, annual donor actually frees a charity up to be more innovative and take more risks rather than chase restricted dollars or the latest trend.

Creating a Plan for Your Everyday Philanthropy

Once you've chosen which programs you want to support, set guidelines for when and how you will donate.

- *Pick your issues proactively* using the tips above. Don't let your big picture be dominated by reacting to requests.

- *Set a budgetary goal* for how much you are aiming to contribute to charities. It might be 5 percent of your gross income, or 10 percent of your take-home pay, or whatever.

If you can, make it a little bit of a stretch goal, perhaps a little more than last year.

- *Have a "pew fund" budget,* of maybe an amount you are comfortable with and will donate to anyone who asks—it could be $20 or $50 or $1,000, if that's where you are, but should be a number that won't eat up too much of your total. Maybe you cap your pew fund at 15 percent or 20 percent of your total giving budget; ideally, that's enough to let you respond to five to ten social requests.

- *Set your donations on autopilot,* and spread them over time to make the effect less noticeable to your budget. Charities run better, and more efficiently, when they have predictable, dedicated support. Not having to chase dollars is what gives their leaders the freedom to pursue new ideas—to be innovative and take risks! Colorado Public Radio (and many other NPR affiliates) uses this approach in their "Evergreen membership"— it's a monthly donation that can be as little as $5 or as much as feels right to you. Personally, I turn down any and all collateral they want to provide as a "thank-you gift"—since those funds come right out of what you just donated and effectively turn it from a donation into a (partial) purchase. If I really want that swag to flex at my next trip to the farmer's market, I add the cost to my donation so they still net the full amount of my intended donation.

- After having experience with an organization and its leadership, add them to your core monthly donation list. Over time, build a cadre of organizations that receive monthly, unrestricted donations from you on autopilot. Ideally this core set of organizations makes up 75 percent or so of your total giving. You know it's on target, you know it's good work, you have it on autopilot and don't have to think about it. Be loyal, be supportive, be low-maintenance for these charities to help them do their best work.

- *Reserve a portion of your giving budget for unexpected events*, like responding to natural disasters or the COVID-19 crisis. This type of giving may also be part of your pew fund.

CONSIDER A DONOR ADVISED FUND

If you haven't built up your monthly donations yet, and you have other reasons for wanting the tax benefits of a charitable deduction, you may want to set up a Donor Advised Fund (DAF). Donor-advised funds are like charitable checking accounts—a 501(c)(3) public charity creates a DAF program and allows you to donate assets into an account that belongs to the charity but which you have advisory privileges over. You can put the money in the DAF now and receive current-year tax benefits, but you don't have to decide which charities receive the funds until later.

There are different flavors of DAF sponsors: *community foundations*, which are typically long-established organizations that benefit a specific geography; *financial institutions*, which are hoping to keep investor dollars in-house, and independent DAFs, which allow donors to invest their assets with the ultimate goal of benefiting a charitable organization. If you want to go this route, do your research and pick a DAF that fits your goals and principles.

If you build up your charitable giving portfolio through the course of the year, you shouldn't have too much left to distribute come year end. But if you do have extra funds you'd like to expend to meet your giving goal, consider using a family holiday gathering like Thanksgiving or Christmas to discuss and make decisions about where to give as a family.

Giving Something Other Than Money

Throughout the year, you can support the charities you've selected with more than just donations: remember to *know your power*—you have other resources besides your checkbook to support the charities you care about. Here are a few other ways to *just give*:

- *Your social networks:* Suggestions from friends and family are one of the most important factors in charitable giving. Your friends know you and trust your judgment, so be an advocate for the causes you care about with friends and family. Online, you can set up a fundraiser for your birthday or another special day, amplify their social media messages, put a URL or sentence about the cause in your personal email signature line, and so on. Offline, make sure your friends and family know of your support for this cause. Ask them to attend events with you or volunteer with you or donate goods. When you donate clothing, ask your friends and family if they have anything to add to the pile, and offer to get them a receipt. Is there some political aspect to the charity's work around which you can rally your friends? Start a petition, write letters, use your influence as a voter, and encourage your neighbors to do the same. At your next social gathering, ask friends to bring a piece of their work wardrobe they no longer wear and donate it to a job training program. Or bring some canned goods that you'll take to the school or neighborhood food pantry.

- *Your purchasing power:* Ask your charity whether there are consumer habits or trends that are affecting them positively or negatively. If you support immigrant rights, be aware of your produce purchases at the grocery store—how was the coffee produced? How was that lettuce harvested? If you give money to a battered women's program, you may want to change your media habits to avoid perpetuating images that portray women as objects and definitely avoid stolen photos, even (especially) if they are "juicy." If you support charities that work to improve the community and provide health care to low-income workers, investigate whether there are certain employers that provide better working conditions and health insurance where you could shop.

- *Your free time:* Are you willing to volunteer your manual labor? Office work, data entry, working at the phone banks? Bring your friends or your spouse or your kids? If you're concerned with animal welfare, be sure your vacations don't harm local ecosystems or animal habitat, or even take a charitable vacation where you spend your time building homes or making improvements in a setting far different from your own. If you support the troops, consider writing letters to those serving abroad.

- *Your employer:* More employers are promoting skills-based volunteering, and your accounting firm may be willing to trade some employee time for community goodwill. They also may be interested in your ideas to boost employee morale: If you're working to *walk lightly*, form a "green committee" to promote "reduce, reuse, and recycle" in the office (the CFO will especially like the "reduce" part in this economy), organize a food drive as part of the annual holiday party, or have the office adopt a few families from a local shelter. Encourage the company to match employee giving.

- *Your stuff:* Goodwill and the Salvation Army aren't the only ones who need gently used stuff: day cares and churches and hospitals need toys, homeless shelters need toiletries, foster kids need backpacks and a few things to call their own. Many charities dislike spending money on office supplies and furniture, so if you have extra pens and notebooks lying around, see if your favorite charities could use them. (One important note: after a natural disaster like flooding, hurricanes, fires, or earthquakes, don't try to send stuff. They can't process it efficiently, and matchmaking is hard. Just donate cash.)

- *Your talents:* Can the charity benefit from any of your skills or talents? If you're a marketer, you could design a logo, or if you're web savvy you could help maintain their website. If you're a writer, you could help with the newsletter. One of my favorite ideas here is to offer your fun talents for the charity auction fundraiser. My mother once worked for a nonprofit that held a live auction each October. Since my husband and I were trained as blackjack and poker dealers in Atlantic City, the charity put together and auctioned off an "In-Home Fish Fry for 20 People" that offered our services combined with those of the family who catered all the local Catholic "Fish Fry" events during Lent. I've never been prouder to help raise $500 for charity, and we all had a blast at the party.

Follow Through

No matter how you pick where to donate, the most important thing is that you *follow through*. If your giving budget is small, don't feel bad. You've activated the rest of your budget to do some of the work that might otherwise be relegated to "discretionary spending"—and you're having more impact than folks who only donate but do nothing else!

CHAPTER 13

Work: Choosing and Influencing Your Workplace

When I was a new entrepreneur in 2012, I was one of the only women tech founders in the buzzy new startup hub in Chicago called 1871. Because of the limited representation of my gender, I was often invited to tours and small meetups with well-known tech founders, investors, and politicians—even some celebrities who were getting into the tech investing scene.

At one event, they asked me to join a meeting with ten other entrepreneurs and the guy who was the CEO of a big, influential tech company that probably has a widget on your smartphone right now. We had the opportunity to ask him questions about his thinking and his management style. One twenty-something male entrepreneur asked, "How do you really get the most out of your developers—like how do you get them to work long hours and really put their heart and soul into the grind for your company?"

I thought the question was problematic enough, since I'm a big believer in work-life balance and had three small children at the time. But the answer was so egregiously discriminatory that my jaw dropped to the floor. He didn't say, "offer them meaningful equity so they participate in the benefits of your success" or "give them a sabbatical or long vacation after a tough stretch so they can reconnect and recharge." No, the CEO said that he had a great tactic to share with them. See, he attended events in the evening a few times a month. And sometimes he would come back to the office after the event ended, about nine or ten o'clock at night. And he'd walk around the office and strike up a conversation with whomever was working in the office at that time to see what they were working on. Then, at the next all-company meeting, he'd be sure to highlight and to praise that work and the people he'd talked to. Mind you, he said, he didn't tell people he would do this or that this was the system for getting his approval, but word would get around that it was beneficial to be working late if he stopped by.

If you are single and childless, this story might not horrify you like it horrified me, a woman with a startup and three young children at home. I could see the problem instantly—people with caregiving responsibilities would never have the ability to stay at the office so late even if they wanted to. I know my own routine was to leave 1871 at 5:00 or 5:30, go home, make dinner, spend time with my husband and kids, and then put them to bed about 8:00 p.m. (the kids, not my husband) before getting back on my computer to work. You wouldn't find me in the office, but that didn't mean I wasn't working long hours to make my startup successful.

The nine other entrepreneurs, all young men, smiled and nodded at how clever this approach was, not recognizing that having a secret code to advancement that can only be fulfilled by a particular segment of your employee base is the same old boys' club, like doing deals over cigars and brandy or a round of golf or a night out at the "gentleman's club." The answer is not to teach women to like cigars and brandy and play golf or be the cool girl who goes along to the strip club. The answer is to have opportunities for recognition and advancement that don't depend on behaviors that are unrelated to job performance (and which are a secret, to boot). Exclusive advancement opportunities are the opposite of shared prosperity.

Today's millennials and younger generations want to work for companies and leaders who care about people, planet, *and* profit— often referred to as a triple-bottom line. Eighty-three percent of Gen Z in the United States consider a company's purpose when deciding where to work.[1] And they are willing to put their money where their mouth is, sacrificing their personal income to work for an aligned company: more than nine out of ten employees are willing to trade a percentage of their lifetime earnings for greater meaning at work.[2] This is more true than ever today, leading to the Great Resignation, as reported by NPR in June 2021:

> People are leaving jobs in search of more money, more flexibility and more happiness. Many are

rethinking what work means to them, how they are valued, and how they spend their time. . . . [A] record 4 million people quit their jobs in April alone.[3]

Employees have recognized that the prosperity they create for their employers is not being equally shared with them and with the community, and they're done having the scales tilted against them. Maybe you're one of these folks and you want to find a company that cares.

But how do you find a socially responsible company to work for? Especially when, as with consumer product marketing, clever organizations have figured out that's what you want and are going to package up their existing culture and benefits and wrap it in the language of social responsibility?

One way that you *used to* be able to differentiate was by working at a nonprofit organization. After all, nonprofits are for doing good, and for profits are for making money, right? As you might imagine, that's not the case anymore. Legal status (nonprofit or for profit) isn't necessarily the best indicator of a company's belief in shared prosperity. I see the universe of companies doing good in two categories: socially responsible companies and social enterprises.

What Is a Socially Responsible Company?

A *socially responsible company* is one whose core business is unrelated to social impact—say photography, carpet cleaning, a shoe company, or an accounting firm—but the business owners and decision makers strive to be socially responsible in how they run all the different aspects of their business. It isn't only about *what* they do, but also *how* they do it. So the photography studio may make sure to pay the creative talent an appropriate wage. The carpet cleaner may use earth-friendly cleaning agents. A shoe company may institute a buy-one, give-one model where each purchase funds a corresponding donation to a person in need. An accounting firm may donate services to a nonprofit chosen by its employees.

Many small business owners are vital members of their local community and strive to be a good neighbor, take care of their employees, and support local schools, parks, and other small businesses. These organizations do not have a legal obligation to integrate social responsibility into their operations (ever heard the saying about how corporations are sociopaths?), but their owners and operators make that choice, and for many it is an important part of their identity.

However, if the business were struggling—struggling to grow, struggling to make a profit, struggling to attract financing—those efforts could always be jettisoned if they were deemed too expensive. Their actions are entirely voluntary, and as such could disappear tomorrow if the winds of fortune or ownership percentages change.

The most committed socially responsible companies may choose to be certified as a *B Corporation* (often called a "B Corp"), which is not a legal status like a C Corporation or a nonprofit. Rather, it's a voluntary designation that can be earned by a company willing to go through a self-evaluation and improvement process. From the B Corporation website:

Certifying as a B Corporation goes beyond product- or service-level certification. B Corp Certification is the only certification that measures a company's entire social and environmental performance. The B Impact Assessment evaluates how your company's operations and business model impact your workers, community, environment, and customers. From your supply chain and input materials to your charitable giving and employee benefits, B Corp Certification proves your business is meeting the highest standards of verified performance.

Positive impact is supported by transparency and accountability requirements. B Corp Certification doesn't just prove where your company excels now—it commits you to consider stakeholder impact for the long term by building it into your company's legal structure.[4]

Examples of B Corps include household names like Patagonia, Ben & Jerry's, Numi tea, New Belgium Brewing, Athleta, Eileen Fisher, Seventh Generation, Better World Books, Happy Family Organics, Namaste Solar, but also law firms, consulting firms, tiny tech startups, and large publishing or media companies. And because B Corp certification is not a legal structure, it's open to companies located anywhere in the world: there are currently more than 3,500 certified B Corporations in seventy countries. Whenever you can, find and support B Corps, because you can feel confident that they have integrated shared prosperity into every part of their business!

What Is a Social Enterprise?

In contrast to the "do good" voluntary actions done by socially responsible companies, a *social enterprise* is a business for which social impact is at the core, baked into the product or company. For example:

- Companies that produce water filters designed to be used in low-income communities and developing countries after natural disasters have polluted water supplies

- A bakery, maintenance shop, or e-commerce fulfillment center that exists as a platform to employ, train, and support returning citizens when they are released from prison so they can transition to a stable and independent life

- A used-clothing business that aims to make buying used clothing as fashionable and as convenient as buying new clothing to break the cycle of fast fashion

For social enterprises, the social impact is the main point, not a side effort, and it is not easy to strip the social impact out of the business—it would become a different business.

In the old days, social enterprises were nonprofits or subsidiaries of nonprofits (for example, New York–based Greyston Bakery, which employs people who have been out of the workforce for some time), but today they can be for profits, especially with some new legal structures: taking the voluntary B Corp status described here one step further, some states have established a new legal structure called a Public Benefit Corporation or Benefit Corporation. These forms differ from traditional corporations in one important way: whose needs get prioritized.

In a traditional corporation, most directors still follow the mandate that the interests of the shareholders are prioritized first, before anyone else, a mandate called "shareholder primacy." As explained by Andrew Ross Sorkin in the *New York Times*, corporate directors' performance is measured by whether they increase shareholder value. Because of the "business judgment rule," they cannot make short-term decisions that fail to maximize value unless they can show that it *will* be maximized in the long term. Writes Sorkin:

> It may be an oversimplification, but if they veer from seeking profits in the name of other stakeholders, shareholders may have a legal case against them. Nowhere in their responsibilities are they expected to consider any stakeholder but the company."[5]

This is why corporations have sometimes been called "sociopaths,"[6] since they do not care for anyone or anything except their own interests.

In a Benefit Corporation, you may legally consider what is in the best interest of other stakeholders, including the employees, the suppliers, the community (and therefore the environment), and the customers. In most cases, you must also publish a publicly available report on your social and environmental performance assessed against a third-party standard.[7] Becoming a Benefit Corporation doesn't mandate different decisions or keep you from making a profit so much as free you from the constraints of a normal corporation that require you to place shareholders above all other stakeholders.

Beyond B Corporation certification or Benefit Corporation status, other tip-offs about a socially responsible company include:

- Where any corporate social responsibility (CSR) efforts sit—somewhere in marketing or reporting to the CEO?

- Same for any diversity, equity, and inclusion efforts—a junior role inside HR or a CEO direct report? Is the company just issuing press releases, or is the CEO a member of public forums discussing issues and working to make improvements?

- A compensation and benefits package that treats employees as whole people with need for a life outside the office. That means health insurance that covers mental health and wellness benefits, adequate time off, and cultural expectations around healthy boundaries (for example, not being expected to respond to emails after hours or on weekends).

In short, look for much of the same criteria it would take the company to become a certified B Corp, even if it hasn't gone through the whole process or didn't quite qualify (like becoming an organic farmer, becoming a B Corp is a challenging and time-consuming process).

Get a Socially Responsible Job

If you're seeking a job that is a boon to the world as well as to yourself, here are a few resources worth checking out:

- Launchpad (https://launchpad.secondday.org): For a comprehensive guide to starting a social impact career, check out Launchpad by Second Day, "your launchpad to a social impact career." They have career guides for everything from government service and fundraising to social enterprises, corporate social responsibility, public health, impact investing, and community organizing. Sign up for a fourteen-day free trial to get access to their list of social impact job boards as well.

- Idealist (https://www.idealist.org): The granddaddy of nonprofit job sites, if more traditional in focusing on nonprofits only. Includes internships, volunteer opportunities, and organization profiles, as well as listings of graduate school fairs and current job openings. Definitely a great resource for those just starting out and looking for a job in the nonprofit sector.

- Impact Opportunity (https://impactopportunity.org): "Impact Opportunity is on a mission to support careers that make a positive impact in the world. We accomplish this by providing a job board, content, and tools to support nonprofits, foundations, and mission-driven companies in building strong teams and individuals pursuing social impact careers and volunteer opportunities."[8]

- Mission Investors Exchange (https://missioninvestors.org/jobs): If you're currently in finance and want to transition to a role in impact investing, MIE is a great hub for these roles.

- Philanthropy News Digest (https://philanthropynewsdigest.org/jobs): Powered by Candid (the organization formed from the merger of the Foundation Center and GuideStar), PND's job board provides listings of current full-time job openings at US nonprofits, foundations, and institutions of higher education.

- Net Impact (https://netimpact.org/jobs): Net Impact's mission is to "inspire and equip emerging leaders to build a more just and sustainable world."[9] Resources include job search tools and tips, career profiles, and a jobs and internships board.

LOOK LOCAL, TOO!

Do a Google search on the terms "nonprofit resources" or "impact careers" and the name of your city, state, or region. You're bound to find a resource center, library,

continued

university, or some other portal that lists local nonprofit jobs. Many metropolitan areas have these kinds of sites, and you're bound to find some local listings, particularly for nonprofits and foundations.

Support an Inclusive Workplace

One key action that everyone can take is supporting an inclusive workplace. That's a term that gets a lot of use these days, but what does it mean to be inclusive? Basically, it means not assuming everyone is like you and therefore making conversational, physical, and emotional space for everyone.

An inclusive space is one where anyone can thrive regardless of differences in age, race, gender, sexual orientation, parental status, physical ability, or other factors that have nothing to do with the ability to do the job.

As a first step toward being inclusive, you need awareness of where you create space and where you make assumptions—you need to see your own Current. Suppose right now it is the Monday after Easter—known to some as "Easter Monday" and to others as simply Monday. If you head into work and ask people how their Easter was, you are not being inclusive because you are assuming the person you are talking to is an active Christian who celebrates Easter.

If you supervise a group of people and reward those who stay in the office late, you aren't creating an inclusive environment for those with caregiving responsibilities, such as parents.

If you attend a social event for the company and ask someone and their spouse when they are planning to have kids, you are assuming they want children, and are able to have them.

To be inclusive is to be curious and open to the possibility that the person in front of you is not the same as you along any one of a number of types of difference. It's not having a default assumption that other people are Christian, heterosexual, want marriage and kids, and so on. That's all. It's not always saying the politically correct statement, it's just leaving space for the possibility of difference. Don't be intrusive with personal questions, and don't assume "people can ask for accommodation"; the trick to being inclusive is not making them raise their hand and ask but caring enough to consider how they might feel comfortable.

As a colleague, a team leader, a manager, or an executive, you can choose to work at being inclusive or you can choose not to make an effort to make everyone feel included and welcome. Here are a few more typical workplace events that provide opportunities to be inclusive, no matter your job:

- Organizing a sales team meeting? Make sure the social activities are accessible to those with physical disabilities.

- Scheduling a big meeting or deadline? Be aware of non-Christian holidays that may limit working hours, like Rosh Hashana, Yom Kippur, Diwali, and Ramadan.

- Have colleagues from other countries or non-white ethnic groups? Make an effort to learn the correct pronunciation of every colleague's name—the way *they* say it themselves.

- Ordering lunch for a group? Include options that accommodate vegetarians or other dietary restrictions.

- Creating web content? Use alt text to describe images for those who have visual impairments.

- Attending a networking event? Don't question people about their drinking choices ("Don't you want a cocktail? Come on, let's relax!"). If you're organizing, make sure there are sober-friendly options besides water.

- Taking a lunch break? Make sure everyone is explicitly invited to join you—especially the newer/junior person.

- Creating an icebreaker? Avoid questions that reveal class status, like hobbies or vacation activities. Try questions about food preferences, pet peeves, a favorite artist or book or movie.

What makes it hard to be inclusive is that we're often not cognizant of how people can be different from us. Personally, I'm hyperaware of ideas that exclude women and parents or assume everyone who lives in Colorado skis or takes international vacations (expensive hobbies, both). I have to work much harder to recognize and avoid the ones that are exclusionary to people of color, immigrants, LGBTQ people, and so on. So, I put in the effort to avoid assumptions, and when I make a mistake (and someone is brave enough to point it out to me), I apologize, make a mental note, and do better the next time.

BE A SPONSOR OR MENTOR, ESPECIALLY TO THOSE WITH LESS ACCESS AND PRIVILEGE

Mentoring someone is when you give them advice and help them learn to navigate the professional world that might be new to them. When someone is the first in their family to go to college, they often don't have the family elder who helps them get through the weird inside world of college applications and classes, internships, resume development, and other white-collar skills, including how to write an introductory email or how to ask a professor for help on an assignment or how to talk to a manager if friction arises. Mentors can help someone navigate these important life skills.

Sponsoring someone is about actively trying to advance their career: Talking them up for assignments and promotions and new opportunities. Making sure they are recognized for their skills whenever opportunities come up. Lots of underestimated people have plenty of mentors but not enough sponsors—people who will use their reputational capital to help them out at work. If you have the opportunity, be a sponsor.

I have observed through my years in startup land that there is a common misconception about what you get when you go to Harvard or Stanford, especially the business schools. I do not believe that you receive an objectively better education at these elite schools; I suspect the curriculum is pretty much the same from one business school to another. Instead, what you receive is admission into an exclusive club of your fellow alumni. Over decades, the alumni of these organizations have supported one another, done deals together, invested in each other, and helped make each other incredibly wealthy. Then they provide warm introductions, the advantage of legacy admissions to attend the school with other alumni children, and prestigious internships with their firms, continuing the cycle.

When someone attends Metro State local community college, they may have great professors and learn great skills. But they don't have an alumni network to vouch for them, to make introductions, and get them into entry-level positions with prestigious firms. They may not have the financial support from their parents to be able to afford to take unpaid internships to gain prestigious firm names on their resume. They may have had to work wherever they could find flexible hours to support their families while going to school at night or on the side.

Looking for prestigious schools, internships, and big-name firms on a resume and calling it "cultural fit" is often a euphemism for seeking folks who come from an upper class, moneyed culture. People who have not attended well-known institutions or have middle-class or wealthy parents often don't have the personal and professional networks to help them along. If you believe in shared prosperity, use whatever access and ability you have to give someone like that a seat at the table.

EVALUATE YOUR COMPANY ON ITS SOCIAL RESPONSIBILITY

If you are "just" an employee, you may feel like you have no role in these issues and don't have any leverage to ask for improvements to the working environment for you and for your fellow employees. But if you can volunteer to be part of the solution, many companies want to take steps to increase employee satisfaction and retention if someone shows them how.

Every company spends money and time and effort in a number of areas, like you do as an individual. I often think of these different areas as a bull's-eye spreading outward from the core (see Figure 1).

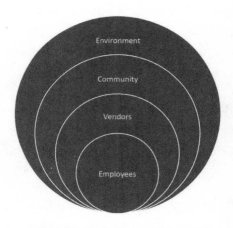

Figure 1: The bull's-eye of impact

To help your company live into the idea of creating shared prosperity, see if you can advocate to improve the way the company furthers prosperity for each group:

Employees

- Does your employer pay living wages for your geography?

- Does your employer offer benefits that provide stability, paid time off, physical and mental health care, opportunities for building wealth (like a 401(k) or profit sharing)? Or do they manipulate part-time hours to prevent people from qualifying for benefits?

- Do they provide a fair and engaging workplace, where difference is celebrated and everyone is evaluated on merit, as reflected in pay and promotions?

- Are your target customers represented in your employee base?

Vendors

- Can you help source local, minority-owned, women-owned, or fair-trade vendors to work with on everything from coffee supplies and office supplies to office artwork or catering?

- Can you introduce them to social enterprises that employ folks trying to develop job skills and build positive work history? Many of these companies exist in food services, property maintenance, customer service, and IT services.

- When holding in-person events, can you encourage them to consider nonprofit community resources like a museum, botanic garden, or community center?

- Do they pay vendors in a timely way to provide critical cash flow for young businesses? Could you encourage longer contract terms to help those businesses with a stable client base and working capital needs?

Community

- Does the company offer pro bono products or services to community organizations? Sponsor kids' schools or sports teams? Could you organize such a donation?

- Do company leaders listen to community voices about important issues that affect them? Are they active on issues that don't directly affect their bottom line but affect the community quality of life?

- Are they making a point to serve low-income members of the community with equal dignity?

- Can you encourage your employer to match employee donations or allow paid volunteer time?

Environment

- Does the company participate in standard environmental practices like recycling and reducing energy usage? Do they try to be a leader and go beyond industry standards?

- Can you organize or join a "green team" to make suggestions and implement solutions across the organization?

- Are there incentives to reduce the impact of commuting on the environment, such as subsidizing public transportation passes, providing bike racks, work-from-home options, or staggered working hours to avoid sitting in traffic?

Arm Yourself with Facts

I wish we could say that companies want to do the right thing so if you just show it to them they will act, but the truth is more like they need to see the financial benefit before committing to do the right thing. So if you want to convince decision makers that it's time to change, come prepared with some facts: Will this cost money in the short term but reap rewards in the medium or long term? How much does employee turnover cost your company now? How loyal are your customers? Could you improve reach into a new customer segment if you had greater representation on a particular outreach or sales or marketing team?

The higher up in a company you are, the more clout you have to make things happen. And many people know deep down this is true, but they perceive they might damage their personal reputation by speaking up for "unpopular" things. They don't want to pay a price for advocating for someone or something that is outside the established archetype. This is where courage and conviction are required—*be brave*, and offer up your status in support of a colleague or an idea.

The good news is, you won't only help them reduce turnover and increase employee loyalty with these actions (including yours!). Research shows purpose-driven companies do better with customers, too: Edelman found in 2018 that 64 percent of people globally expect CEOs to lead on social change,[10] and Porter Novelli reports that "Americans say it is more critical than ever to buy from companies that reflect their personal values—and they believe supporting these companies is a way to show they care about issues that are important to them."[11]

CHAPTER 14

Celebrate: Create Moments That Reflect Your Values

Yesterday is history. Tomorrow is a mystery.
But today is a gift. That's why it's called the present.

—MASTER OOGWAY, *KUNG FU PANDA*

When it comes to celebrating special moments and the people we love with parties or gifts, it is easy to give ourselves a pass on many otherwise important values, especially *walking lightly in this world.* I've found that weddings and baby showers, in particular, justify all kinds of excess and waste that we otherwise might avoid. But with a little bit of a different mindset—with a focus on presence over presents—it doesn't have to be that way.

I like to think of celebrations and special occasions as marking a given day with gratitude. We are grateful for having another person in our life, and we take time to express that gratitude on the day they were born and, in the case of a spouse, the day we married. We mark occasions to celebrate the eternal love of God—we can be grateful for the gift of salvation or the gift of spring renewal and new beginnings. We are grateful and bear witness to special moments in someone's life, including graduations and religious milestones. Sometimes, we're grateful just to know and spend time with someone special.

Whether you're planning a wedding, celebrating a birthday, or welcoming a new family member, the way we choose to share our joy is an important reflection of who we are and what we value. There's nothing wrong with spending money to celebrate special events, but our moments together are most special when we think of those entertainment and celebration dollars as tools we have to express our gratitude *and* our values, rather than a reason to set them aside.

A New Perspective on Gift Giving

I remember when my children were little, it seemed like no matter how hard we tried, we couldn't reduce the amount of stuff they received for every occasion. This is a very #FirstWorldProblem, where your kids have more toys than they need, but one that many parents face. And frankly, as consumer goods continue to get cheaper, it isn't necessarily a sign of having a lot of money to have a lot of stuff come your way at every holiday—from Valentine's Day to birthdays to Christmas or Hannukah or other special occasions. Thanks in part to the consumption industry telling us we should mark every named occasion with a card and a gift, we feel obliged to give presents at every turn. Perhaps it's no surprise those presents have also gotten cheaper and less meaningful over time.

For many years, when my kids came down the stairs on Christmas morning, they would have presents from my husband and me, from grandparents, from aunts and uncles, and even from nonrelated friends and other adults. Even if we tried to limit the number of presents under the tree from us and Santa, by the time all these others were added, the tree was overflowing through the living room. But it never felt right, especially when they were more interested in the wrapping paper and the cardboard boxes than the gifts themselves. Talk about an embarrassment of riches.

Outside of special occasions, they would bring home candy, fidget toys, erasers, plastic sunglasses, bouncy balls, stickers, and other assorted Happy Meal toys from school, from the dentist, from other kids' birthday parties (blast you, parent who invented "goody bags"!), and so on.

How do you change this dynamic, where your home serves as a short pit stop between a plastics factory and the dump? Here are my general guidelines for celebrations and gifts for every age.

- *Give them experiences instead of stuff.* Hands down, I think this is the best option to avoid unnecessary consumption and *walk lightly*. If the experience itself is socially responsible—such as a farm-to-table restaurant that avoids waste and pays living wages—so much the better. Either way, now you have a new memory that will last forever and never get taken to the charity thrift store.

- *Give local food.* I also place a high value on giving great food and beverage gifts made locally that will be treasured as a special treat—including artisan meats and cheeses, gourmet chocolate or a unique beer, wine, or spirit from a local producer.

- *Give to charity in someone else's name.* Giving to a friend's or family member's favorite charity is often seen as a luxury by them, and it makes us feel good, two great attributes for any gift. Find a charity already supported by the person you want to honor, and make a gift in their name. Or make a donation that honors an interest or skill of your loved one. For example, if someone is handy at home renovation, donate to Habitat for Humanity in their name. If you don't know the person's favorite charity, you can use a service that allows your recipient to choose the ultimate beneficiary of the donation, such as Charity Choice (https://charitygiftcertificates.org; your recipient selects the charity) or Kiva (https://kiva.org; they select the loan recipients).

- *Pay it forward.* What life lessons, skills, and so on did you learn from the person you want to honor? You have so many nonmonetary assets that you can use to help someone else and then share your story with the gift recipient. Maybe you could mentor a student like they mentored you. Or volunteer in a food pantry to feed others the way they nurtured you. Volunteer and then write a note to the honoree explaining your actions and how they inspired you.

- *Help them learn and grow.* Donate to a 529 college fund for a young person. Pay for a class that you can do together or otherwise help them get training in a topic related to their favorite hobby or future career interest. For young families, help with extracurricular activities can really lighten their load.

- *Give them gifts that are homemade.* Those handprint ornaments are always the most fun to look at and remember each year when we do our Christmas tree. My dad still has a blue ombre change holder on his dresser that I made for him in high school ceramics. But if you think homemade gifts are just for kids, think again. Turn your hobby into a special gift for teachers, neighbors, coworkers, or your holiday party host. Bake, sew, craft, ferment, grow, or otherwise create something unique with your own hands. Even better if your materials are sourced ethically—for example, organic yarn, recycled glass, or produce from your garden or a farm stand.

- *Give gift certificates.* One way to avoid buying gifts that the recipient won't use is to buy gift certificates so the person can buy something they want. Can you use a gift certificate to introduce them to a great B Corp they might not already know? Or a great local restaurant, spa, book store, or other local business that could use the support?

- *If you want to buy stuff, do so responsibly.* If you want to give physical gifts, look for artisan (hello Etsy!), fair trade, green, or otherwise socially responsible items. Buy local if you can, and make sure that what you buy aligns with the values of your gift recipient. For example, when buying a physical gift for my mother, I would seek out companies that employ women, pay them a fair wage, provide decent benefits, have women in positions of power, and so on.

With these guidelines in mind, let's talk about how they translate to some of our most common celebrations, whether you are the one being celebrated or you are celebrating someone else.

START A FOUNDATION

My father is the type who doesn't need much, and he doesn't want anything he doesn't need. For a few years, I tried valiantly to come up with Christmas and birthday gifts he might appreciate: a car emergency kit that he keeps in his trunk still feels like a small victory.

He turned sixty a few years ago. Instead of a package, I decided to set up a foundation. I told him, "I know you've always said that if you win the lottery, you would start a foundation. Well, I'm thinking your chances aren't so hot. But since I work in philanthropy—and I won the 'Lottery of Birth'—I'm starting a family foundation with you as the president. It won't be big, dollar-wise. But I realized recently that legacy is cumulative."

I named my mom and siblings and myself as codirectors. Now, years later, the adult members of our family don't exchange Christmas presents or birthday presents. We contribute to the foundation. We all still have our personal giving, but deciding on gifts out of the foundation is a group effort.

If something like this is appealing, but you think a foundation is for the Gateses and Buffets, you'll be excited to know that many financial institutions offer a donor-advised fund that you can start with just $5,000 (pool resources with other family members?). Ask your financial advisor about your options.

Kids' Birthdays

The irony about young kids' birthday parties is that they rarely remember the first few, so the celebration is more about us than them. As they get older, they're likely to remember the event more than any particular gift (unless you actually buy them that pony, I suppose). Here are some ideas to create memories of the celebration and beyond.

- Ballet lessons, music lessons, gymnastics class, or any "mommy and me" (or "daddy and me") classes create learning for kids and special time for parents. If you want something to wrap up, think of any special items needed for class (like a leotard or maracas).

- If you live in or near a big city, take a ride downtown on the train and have lunch or tea at a local landmark or unique restaurant. Even if it's just the regional commuter rail, kids love trains!

- Go to a minor league ballgame where you can get affordable seats close to the action. Arrive early to get autographs; kids are great at scoring signatures from these future major leaguers!

- If you live close enough, take a trip to the beach or boardwalk and get some ridiculous ice cream concoction. There's no need for special toys, but a bucket and shovel to make sandcastles together creates many fun memories.

- A membership to the zoo, museum, botanic garden, aquarium, or other family-friendly amenity is a gift that the family can use all year.

- When kids are really young (and unlikely to remember much), you can also give them a strong start with a gift to a savings account or to establish a 529 for their future education.

- If you are the one hosting a birthday party for a young person, try not to create a lot of waste with single-use plastics, plates, cups, decorations, and so on. In our house, we have two or three "Happy Birthday" signs that we rotate and use year after year.

- Sending out invitations? If you feel your child doesn't need additional gifts from friends and family, consider adding language like "Please, no presents; it is a gift just to celebrate with you!"

- Instead of goody bags that are destined for the junk drawer, one year we took pictures of each guest with the birthday child at arrival. We had a little photo printer and were able to print them while the party was in progress and attach them to a paper "friends" frame to hand out as they headed home. If you don't have a photo printer, you can take them on your phone and use an app to submit to a one-hour print service; someone can run to the drugstore and pick them up before cake is served.

- To help every child leave with something they can be excited about (that isn't plastic), ask everyone to wrap up a favorite book, leave it on a table, and have guests grab a new title on their way out.

Adult Birthdays

When you're celebrating an adult birthday, there are a ton of options to create a special experience for everyone.

- Take everyone to a favorite hiking spot or meet up for a bike ride along a scenic route. Stop at a local place to eat, or bring a picnic basket to enjoy.

- Pick something you/they love and go see how it's made. My husband is a big fan of craft beers, so we've been to several brewery tours. But we've also been to candy factories, woolen mills, and artisan workshops. If you do purchase a gift after the tour, you will feel good about knowing how it was made and the local creators that you are supporting with your purchase.

- Get tickets to a special event. My husband got me tickets to see Maroon 5 and we danced so much my Fitbit registered three hours of "active minutes"! For Christmas the following year he got me tickets to see Michelle Obama on her book tour.

- Arrange to take a fun class together, like a dance lesson, painting session, or maker workshop. For my mom's birthday, my sister got her a cooking lesson and they learned to make empanadas from scratch.

- Make and share your specialty. My friend Tracey doesn't like people recognizing her birthday, so I kept it super simple and made her my homemade watermelon jalapeño margaritas in a mason jar and a batch of our family recipe raisin bran muffins that she loves.

- If you're the one celebrating, use the occasion to ask friends and family on social media or electronic invitations to support your favorite charity. Many platforms have made it easy to collect donations, and you would be surprised who might contribute a few bucks to help a cause you care about.

Additions to the Family (Birth and Adoption)

When a family adds a new child, you can help the family get a great start together and be creative in meeting their needs without adding to the unnecessary consumption.

Babies outgrow many items before they wear them out. One of the best things you can do is get gently used items, including cribs, changing tables, rocking chairs, and yes, clothing. Offer to accompany the expecting parents to hunt for great finds from craigslist, flea markets, and consignment stores, and if you're really a great friend, help them clean it up and get ready for baby.

Toys can be sanitized and passed on, too, though probably not those made of cloth that can't be washed, or teething toys. When she was expecting, my cousin asked for books that our kids had loved when they were little, and it gave us a great excuse to purge our bookshelves and pass along some favorites like *Knuffle Bunny* and *The Book with No Pictures* instead of sending them to a thrift store.

- If you don't live close by, consider sending cash or a gift certificate to a world-positive baby brand like Honest, Seventh Generation, or Earth Mama Organics to help them discover safe, healthy, and eco-friendly baby products.

- Give new parents the gift of time. Bring meals that they can easily heat up during those first days with a new baby. Prepay a cleaning service for a few weeks when they won't be able to face scrubbing the bathroom. If you visit them, don't create extra work by making them host you. Take the initiative to pick up toys, bring or help prepare food, maybe even run a few errands.

- If the parents are into nutrition, consider a small blender or food processor that is designed to make quick work of pureeing fruits and vegetables for healthy meals. Ideally, the appliance would not be made of plastic or would at least be BPA-free. Include a recipe book or tips and tricks to help them get started.

- If you're hosting a baby shower, use local and underrepresented vendors for catering, cakes, and decorations. Avoid single-use plastics and waste. If you don't want to have it in your home, consider a nonprofit or small business venue such as a botanic garden, a manicured park, a historic property, art gallery, or rooftop garden. You can search Peerspace's website (https://www.peerspace.com) by city and type of venue to find unique options near you.

Weddings

If you get married, chances are good that your wedding is the biggest party you will ever personally host. Infuse your charitable impulses into your family traditions right from the start. There are many ways to have a fantastic celebration to start off your integrated life with a new partner.

- If you and your future spouse are combining households rather than just starting out, there is often no real need for linens or dishes. In lieu of a traditional wedding registry, you could offer guests the opportunity to donate to a charity that is meaningful to you. Or to fund a dream honeymoon.

- Have the wedding shower and/or reception at a local museum, zoo, theater, botanic garden, or other venue operated by a nonprofit. It will have plenty of natural beauty, and the funds from hosting such events provide much-needed earned income to these organizations.

- Give a donation to charity and provide a small acknowledgment card for each guest rather than buying tchotchkes with ribbons that match the bridesmaids' dresses (hey, the font color can match the bridesmaids' dresses instead).

- Donate cut flowers to a nursing home after the wedding; use plants rather than cut flowers for centerpieces, and find a great place to plant them afterward (like the front lawn of your new home together) or send them home with your guests.

- Ask the caterer to donate unused food to a local food pantry or shelter. Most states have so-called "Good Samaritan" laws that protect those making donations of food so caterers can be confident their good deed won't come back to bite them.

- Use socially responsible vendors and social enterprises where you can. For example, serve fair trade coffee, hire a caterer who is a person of color, or put folks up at a local bed and breakfast or boutique hotel instead of a national chain (so profits stay in the community rather than heading back to corporate headquarters).

- Bridesmaids not attending another black tie event soon? Maybe they want to donate their dresses. There are charities that take these dresses and give them to high school girls who can't afford to buy one. Search for "donate wedding dresses" or "donate prom dresses" to find some options in your area.

- And of course, go green on wedding supplies, like using recycled paper for invitations (which can have a very boutique, cultured look).

GETTING STARTED:
SELECT A CAUSE AS A COUPLE

How does a couple begin to select the causes or charities that should receive donations from their wedding? A colleague once told me the story of one couple who wanted to honor the bride's mother, who had died of breast cancer. You might think they chose a breast cancer charity. But they didn't want to focus on the illness that claimed her life at the very end. She had breast cancer, but that's not the person that she was. Instead, they chose to donate to a charity she felt passionate about, one working to save the manatees.

If you do not have a special charity like that to honor, your wedding may be a great opportunity for you to start thinking about your shared identity and passions. I would encourage you to pick something that resonates with both of you, something you can see getting involved with, together, rather than choosing a charity that only one of you is involved in and passionate about.

Mother's Day and Father's Day

As a mother of three myself, I have come to love Mother's Day. But I can also confirm the old saying: when your kids are little, all you want for Mother's Day is some time to yourself. When your kids are older, all you want is time together. I'm definitely in the "time together" camp now that my kids are teenagers.

If you want to let your parents know you appreciate them, focus on something they love, or something they taught you, or something that captures your shared history. I think showing our parents how they have influenced us to be good people is the best expression of gratitude and will bring them the greatest joy.

- My cousins bought their mother a service that helps you capture and share your life story and turn it into a book. It sends the person a writing prompt each week, like "What is your earliest memory?" After a year, the company binds up all the stories and sends you a book of memories written by your loved one.

- My dad is hard to shop for, and he has a tremendous heart for people in need. I often pick a charity that helps people who are struggling and make a donation in his name.

- For Father's Day, we always took my husband strawberry picking at a local farm, came home with a bushel or two of strawberries, and used it to make his favorite—homemade strawberry jam that lasted until the following year *and* could be a good host gift if we went to a friend's house for dinner. (My husband wants you to know it was actually him who made the jam out of the strawberries we picked. In any case, he loved that jam, so it was still a present for him, right?)

- Last year for Christmas, I subscribed us to a mystery game company that sends out a new mystery each month so that my mom and sisters and I can all play online together and have a reason to connect. We learned our love of games from my mother, who subscribed to *Games* magazine all through our childhood.

Romantic Partners

If there's anyone for whom you should put time and effort into selecting a gift or planning a celebration, it's your chosen life partner. Shared history, including shared struggles, has a special meaning with your chosen family.

- A few years ago, I had our oldest daughter design us a simple family crest and got it made into temporary tattoos for our anniversary—one for us and each of our three kids. We all had matching tattoos on the inside of our wrists for two weeks.

- That same year, my husband took me to a wine-tasting room where you could also make your own wine and bottle it and design the label. Six weeks later we went back and bottled thirty bottles of a sweet, very average red with the label designed by our oldest daughter that included that same family crest and "Schneider Family Vineyard, est. 2000" (the year we were married).

- For our parents' anniversary one year, my sister arranged for a photographer to come and take family photos of us when we were all together at Thanksgiving.

- Back in the day, my husband used to make me mix tapes for road trips. Actually, I'm not *that* old; they were burned onto CDs. But when a song from one of those mix tapes comes on the radio today, we both just look at each other with a little smile. Maybe the modern equivalent is a Spotify playlist?

Other Holidays

- For housewarming, consider gifting a plant instead of a decorative item that might not match their style. Or maybe a young tree they could plant in the yard to mark the passage of years together.

- When a family member hits an important milestone, like graduation and moving out of the house, put together a collection of family recipes so they can take a little bit of home (and a lot of memories) with them.

- When my oldest was little, she took art classes every week for a few years. At the holidays, I would scan in twelve of the best drawings and use an online photo software program to turn them into a calendar for the following year, which made a great gift for the extended family. My sister did something similar with family photos.

Celebrating an Integrated Life

What these celebration ideas have in common is that they take some thought, some time, and some effort. The Current tells you to grab something from the store—just pick one of the "10 Gifts Every Woman in Your Life Will Love!" The more you spend, the more you must love the person, right? Nah, of course not.

What gives gifts true power and meaning is not their price tag but their specific meaning to the recipient. Celebrations and gifts can show people that we see them, and know them, and value them enough to make a special choice, to arrange a special event, or to spend our time and effort to create an item or a memory that reflects our relationship.

And if you don't have the time, money, or other resources to create a special event or item, write a letter or a card that sincerely and thoughtfully tells the person you're honoring how much they mean to you. I guarantee, it will be absolutely treasured and have the desired effect of showing them how special they are to you.

CHAPTER 15

Relationships: Strengthen Your Connections with Partners and Children

I t is sometimes easier to be friendly to relative strangers: having guests over means we are all on our best behavior; those first few dates with a new person are marked with excitement and positive emotions, and we put in the extra effort to make a positive impression.

But when we're in a long-term relationship with someone, whether a parent, child, romantic partner, or just a friend, that euphoric feeling wears away and we aren't always our best selves. How do we include our personal relationships as an expression of our commitment to an integrated life? How do we make sure that the people we value most are also the recipients of our intentions for a better world?

Relationship researcher John Gottman found a succinct way to describe the everyday moments in our relationships that provide opportunity to connect with the people you love. He describes those opportunities as "bids": one person makes a bid (big or small) for connection, whether a touch or an audible sigh or a question like "How was work?" If the other person accepts the bid and gives their attention, Gottman calls this "turning toward" your partner. Or they can "turn away" by missing or ignoring the bid, or even react in hostility, thereby "turning against" their partner.[1]

In just one dinner conversation, individuals may make up to one hundred bids. In healthy relationships, says Gottman, the partners accept the vast majority of bids, at 86 percent. In unhealthy relationships, only 33 percent of the bids are accepted.

Gottman was talking about romantic partners, but I think the idea holds true for all kinds of relationships. To be a good partner, friend, coworker, and parent comes down to putting in the work to be mentally present and authentic in our interest in others. This isn't about making polite small talk with your neighbors or asking you to "be nice" with every person you meet (though that's not a bad idea). It's about real caring, which leads to real connection.

The good news is that many of the tenets of an integrated life help us find authentic connection with others.

- *Embrace "yes, and."* If your partner makes a small gesture of caring, take a moment to acknowledge and appreciate it, even if everything else in your relationship isn't perfect. That's the "yes" part. Then follow up with an "and" with another gesture.

- *Just give.* Don't wait for the perfect moment to start giving your time and attention. If you're immersed in your phone and your partner makes a bid, accept it and turn toward them. Consistently accept their bids with enthusiasm, even if at first you feel like you're the only one doing the "turning toward." (If they don't reciprocate relatively quickly, though, maybe give to someone who will?)

- *Be brave.* Making a bid is often subtle (a look, a sigh) because being subtle protects us from putting ourselves out there in an obvious way and facing potential rejection. But *being brave* means we are vulnerable enough to ask our partners, loved ones, and friends for what we need.

- *Resist the allure of convenience.* Sometimes it just feels easier to spend our precious free time focused on logistics, like where to meet, what to eat, and who is responsible for what. In addition to those logistics, spend time connecting, even when it's not convenient.

Though these ideas apply to *all* relationships, there are two that often become critical in our daily lives and in our overall ability to feel we are living an integrated life: the relationship we have with our romantic partner and the one we have with our children.

Negotiate a Balanced Relationship with Your Partner

At the office, women may be the CEO or the assistant, but most of society assumes we are CEOs of our own households. If your oldest goes to school without her hair brushed, others instinctively think Mom wasn't on her game this morning; if another parent wants to arrange a play date or see why you haven't RSVP'd to the birthday party, they call or email Mom. A few years ago, blogger M. Blazoned dubbed this being the "default parent."[2]

And most of the time women accept it. We take responsibility for responding to all birthday party invitations, choosing, acquiring, and wrapping an appropriate gift and either driving or arranging a ride. Mothers are usually the ones who send notes to the teachers, pack or order school lunches, and keep track of when the art show is taking place next spring so that we don't schedule something on top of it.

Luckily, my husband is as supportive of me as I could ever have asked from a life partner. Still, he sometimes feels like I am constantly asking him to do things, always adding to his "honey-do list." To give him full credit, he has almost always taken on 50 percent of the work, including laundry and yard work, and entertaining or driving the kids. But during the early years of our marriage, it tended to be 50 percent that was pure manual labor. His muscles are undeniably fantastic, but it was his brain that I wanted.

And most women aren't lucky enough to have a partner who takes on 50 percent of the work to keep the household functioning. As the pandemic hit, the gender gap in terms of childcare and household chores only worsened.[3]

While younger men may be more likely to say they believe in equality between the sexes, a Gallup poll found that "among opposite-sex couples, those ages 18 to 34 were no more likely than older couples to divide most household chores equitably."[4] Interestingly, same-sex couples tend to divide household labor more evenly, because "they don't have traditional gender roles to fall back on,"[5] in order to predetermine who should be doing what.

Women in the workplace have paid the price for this extra burden at home: "Mothers suffer a penalty relative to non-mothers and men in the form of lower perceived competence and commitment, higher professional expectations, lower likelihood of hiring and promotion, and lower recommended salaries."[6] Thus, the gender pay gap.

To overcome these disadvantages and create a fair playing field for all, equitably sharing household responsibilities with your partner is one of the most fundamental ways to advance shared prosperity. If you both have careers you care about, sharing the burden at home gives you both the opportunity to spend equal time advancing those careers and still have leisure time for rest, hobbies, and fun.

As a working mother, I used to wonder how I could ask more effectively for the help I needed. I didn't want to fall into the stereotype of a nagging wife. I didn't want to have a petty argument about who does more around the house, since my husband was undeniably doing a lot. What I needed was for him to make more decisions and oversee entire sections of our household operations, from planning to execution.

One night about ten years ago, I asked him to sit down with me to talk about managing our changing schedules and workloads. Together, we brainstormed six discrete areas of the household that required constant management and oversight. Here are the six household "job positions" that we defined that night:

- *Executive chef:* Planning for the week ahead, securing ingredients, preparing meals/snacks, and ordering or packing school lunches. Cooking dinner most nights, or arranging for it to be cooked or otherwise procured via takeout or dining in a restaurant.

- *Facilities manager:* Keeping the inside of the house (relatively) clean and straightened and putting in a special effort when company is expected. This includes laundry, mopping the floor, dusting, and vacuuming and cleaning the bathrooms, as well as seasonal tasks like changing air filters and window screens. Calling and managing all contractors, handling any repairs directly or through the landlord.

- *Chief financial officer:* Paying the bills, doing taxes, handling insurance and investments and 401(k)s, overseeing legal matters like wills and managing the family budget.

- *Chief medical officer:* Making and keeping appointments for well-baby visits and annual physicals, making and keeping dental appointments, getting forms filled out for sports and camp, picking up prescription refills, and making sure over-the-counter medications are on hand. (In families with chronic or serious health issues, this role is enormous.)

- *Dean of students:* Overseeing and checking all homework, handling all correspondence and interactions with school and childcare providers, including curriculum nights, parent/teacher conferences, changes in schedule, making alternate arrangements when there are random days off school, signing kids up for and managing participation in extracurriculars, including transportation or carpool arrangements.

- *Head groundskeeper:* Maintaining the outside of the house, including grass, landscaping, gutters, garage, sidewalk, trash and recycling bins, and outdoor toys.

I'm sure we could have come up with more—maybe "cruise director" in charge of creating and maintaining a social life and celebrations, or "crew chief" tasked with keeping vehicles cleaned, maintained, filled with gas, and repaired as necessary—but six was a nice, even number to start with. We each picked three we were willing to manage and did a hand-off of the pertinent information, contacts, and procedures associated with our new areas of responsibility.

When we first came up with that list, my husband (whose teaching schedule often allowed him to arrive home before me) became the executive chef; though he might ask me to pick up some milk on the way home, he would never look at me when

I walked through the door at 5:30 and ask, "What's for dinner?" And when he decided that we were having fish sticks and macaroni and cheese for dinner (which I despise), I just said, "Thank you."

See, that's the part that makes this work. If he's going to be the responsible party, I have to accept his definition of "good enough." If he's acting as the facilities manager and he doesn't fold the kids' clothes the way I would, I am not going to refold them. If he doesn't put the pasta in the "right" place in the pantry, I don't move it.

If you want to try this, you have to let go of the way *you* would do the job positions that you are not responsible for. If you can't do that, maybe you should take charge of that particular area of responsibility. And if that means you end up overseeing all areas of responsibility once again, then you have no one to blame but yourself.

Now, in 2021, our kids are teenagers and a lot more helpful around the house. My still-amazing husband is now at home with the kids while I am working full time. I'm still our family chief financial officer but have taken on executive chef and play a supporting VP role to his lead on the other areas.

I have often said that for an ambitious woman, her choice of life partner is one of the most consequential decisions she'll ever make. Whether you are that woman, or you are in a relationship with one, I encourage you to find a system that prioritizes your interests and ambitions equally with your partner's.

Influencing and Supporting Your Children's Journeys

When it comes to kids, every parent has seen their child mimic something they do (especially if by "something" you mean repeat a bad word you said in front of them). By the time your kids are old enough to talk and walk, people might be telling you how much they look like you (my kids all inherited the annoying cowlick smack dab on the back of my head) and how they have your mannerisms or speech patterns.

Other habits we transmit can be harder to spot. But kids miss nothing—they learn simply by watching us. It's no surprise that kids mimic how their parents treat people (so you better believe I am respectful and appreciative to essential workers, before, during, and after a pandemic!).

Recently a friend of mine named Barry told me the story of how his grown daughters spent their COVID-19 relief "stimmies" (stimulus checks, for the unhip people out there). One daughter used it to replace her old computer, which she needed for school and work. The other, still employed throughout the pandemic, said she didn't need the money and donated it to the local food bank. Barry was astounded and wondered as he relayed the story to me, "Where did she get that idea?" And I laughed at him and quoted the old "Just Say No" public service announcement: "She learned it by watching *you*!" Barry and his wife had been working on social issues like environmental conservation for their entire careers. Their professional lives revolved around the idea that we have to think beyond ourselves to the whole ecosystem and create something that works for everyone. They had donated to charities, volunteered time, and lived their lives in accordance with those values. It wasn't a wonder to me at all where she got that idea.

Walk the Walk

If you are trying to be conscious about raising charitable and socially conscious children, you need to have conversations with them along the way. But you need to do more than tell them; you need to *show* them how you are living your values.

Of course, you're showing them your values in your efforts to live an integrated life every day. But if you want them to internalize gratitude and community-building behaviors, you need to be explicit about helping others. My own parents involved us regularly in their volunteer efforts.

- They signed us up to make casseroles and bring side dishes when it was our church's week to stock the local homeless shelter with a hot meal. We'd help with the cooking and many times rode along with my mom as she delivered them to the shelter.

- We volunteered at Habitat for Humanity, where I learned much more than how to swing a hammer (and the first nonprofit board I ever joined was the local Habitat for Humanity affiliate in my hometown).

- My dad was a notoriously easy mark for neighborhood fundraisers. You came to the door selling candy bars for your sports team? He'd take five. Girl Scout at the grocery store? He had ten boxes at home (courtesy of his three daughters), but he would take a few more Thin Mints just to be supportive. A kid with a cause is kryptonite to my dad, in the best possible way.

- They were volunteer coaches for our school sports teams and spent hours every year teaching us about basketball, soccer, T-ball, and more. We learned how to play (poorly), and we learned to be good sports (pretty well). My father's mantra was that "we root *for* our team, not *against* the other team."

- My mom volunteered with my Girl Scout troop, leading our efforts to earn the "Marian Award" in eighth grade. She was the "cookie mom" a few years as well, a job I took up when my own daughter was a Girl Scout thirty years later.

- My dad (an MBA and CPA by training) was the treasurer for the high school band association, while my sisters and I went through the color guard and dance corps. Even after we graduated, he still showed up to support the high school athletes and the booster's fundraising events.

- After years in higher education, my mother went to work for a nonprofit serving extremely low-income people and taught us about their mission, their operations, and their impact on the community.

- Even now in retirement, my father volunteers with a charity that assists adults with Down syndrome or other health issues that affect their independence. He reconciles their bank accounts each month.

Kids remember this stuff, and showing care for others makes a huge impression on them. I have taught my kids that same mantra about rooting *for*, not against. But I've also tried to live a life of service to others, following the example that my parents set for me.

Frankly, with all the bad news coming our way lately about suffering in the world, there are a lot of problems that kids might feel anxious about, just like you and me. As adults, we need to find ways to help kids take action and have control over something in order to encourage agency and resilience. People always recite that quotation from Fred Rogers: "When I was a boy and I would see scary things in the news, my mother would say to me, 'Look for the helpers. You will always find people who are helping.'"[7] What has always bothered me about that quotation is that it is missing the action step: don't just *look* at those helpers; *be* a helper yourself! We can show our kids that when you find the helpers, join them. Do what you can, where you are, with what you have. Hopefully they will discover that helping others is like therapy to heal our own fear and pain.

Some ideas we've tried with our own family include fundraisers, volunteering, and donating.

- My daughter once commented about the number of homeless people we saw on the corners when we moved to Denver. She wanted to do something to help, so we made up some brown paper bags with new socks, hand wipes, water bottles, and snacks to hand out when we saw someone on the corner. She even asked our dentist if he had some toothpaste samples, and he gave her about one hundred mini tubes and toothbrushes to include. We kept them in the car, and if we saw someone standing on the corner panhandling, one of the kids would offer them a bag.

- When my niece was six, she had the idea to sell water to people attending the neighborhood garage sale and donate the proceeds to our church's emergency fund. Her parents bought the water, she sold it for $1 a bottle, and all proceeds went to the emergency fund.

- After Hurricane Harvey, my daughter Audrey wanted to send money to the people in Houston, and her baking and cupcake decorating skills are on point. So we made samples for the neighbors and posted on the local Facebook page and sold and baked a bunch of beautiful cupcakes. She raised $400 with her efforts, and we sent it to the mayor of Houston to help the people affected by the storm.

- At Christmas a few years ago, there was a big gap between what I had intended to donate to charity and what we still had left in the budget. And we were all bothered about things happening in our country, like kids being separated from their parents at the border, plastic choking the oceans, and natural disasters destroying people's homes. So we talked it through as a family. We decided together on the issues we wanted to support, and I found local charities for their approval. The kids were so compassionate in their choices, it made me incredibly proud. And I know they felt better having made a contribution to the solution.

- To help abused animals, we gave to the Dumb Friends League.

- To bolster support for immigrants, the Rocky Mountain Immigrant Advocacy Network.

- For helping people become educated and registered to vote, the League of Women Voters.

- For trying to save our polluted oceans, the Ocean Cleanup Project.

- And for people affected by natural disasters (increasingly caused by climate change), World Central Kitchen, led by Chef José Andrés.

- We had a major spring break trip get cancelled at the beginning of the pandemic, and I got a refund of a few thousand dollars for our flights, hotel, and activities planned. I talked with my husband and kids, and we decided together to donate it all to the Rocky Mountain Food Bank—we could see people needed food assistance a lot more than we needed a vacation.

YOUR KIDS ARE WATCHING

If you think your efforts with your kids don't matter, I want to show you why you're wrong. On my father's sixtieth birthday, I wrote a letter to him explaining just a small part of how he had influenced me as a person and as a parent:

"I have such strong memories of you and Mom from as far back as I can remember helping other people. Habitat for Humanity, St. Vincent de Paul, the Dakota Center, making casseroles for the men's shelter . . . the list goes on. The strong moral compass that you and Mom instilled in us has been an important and guiding force in all our lives.

"I look at our family and I'm so proud of the strong relationships we have, and the people we have become. If, as you've told me, you're proud of the way we are raising your grandchildren, it's because I had exceptional models to follow. Some people want to be nothing like their parents—I want to be just like mine."

I hope someday my own kids write me a letter like that.

Sharing Prosperity through Human Relationships

Most of the time when people speak about "prosperity," they mean wealth or status or material goods. In the integrated life, prosperity has a much broader meaning. It includes the prosperity of having a healthy environment and walking more lightly in the world. It also includes the prosperity represented by having supportive and authentic connections to other human beings, and especially those we are closest to.

If you have a life partner and/or children, you know that the stresses of everyday living can sometimes keep us from paying attention to the richness that these relationships bring into our lives. I hope you will join me in trying to become more conscious of the "bids" that are made toward us and responding with loving attention as often as we can to our partners, children, and any other people in our lives. That, to me, is as much a part of having an integrated life as any other actions we might take.

CHAPTER 16

Community: Getting Better Together

Win/Win is based on the paradigm that there is
plenty for everybody, that one person's success is not achieved
at the expense or exclusion of the success of others.

—STEPHEN COVEY, *THE 7 HABITS OF
HIGHLY EFFECTIVE PEOPLE*

Last fall I was invited to participate in a month-long work-shop exploring models of shared ownership, organized by Community Cooperative and the Community Purchasing Alliance. The workshop was taught in a way that reflected the values of the cooperative movement: different members of the leadership team took turns diving deep with us on content to set the table for the week's conversations, and then we spent a significant amount of time in a small peer group exploring ideas and applying them to our own professional (but also personal) lives. It was powerful for me to spend that time reflecting on how I wanted to build my future as a member of community and not a "sole contributor," isolated leader, or siloed employee.

In this workshop, during a writing exercise where we imagined a day five years into our future, I realized that the life I wanted to live would be seamless between my values and my professional work. That full alignment was my number-one priority for imagining a peaceful and fulfilling future. I did not want to take first and then give back a portion; I wanted to give all along the way and trust that the universe will provide, that my community will provide. My mantra became *be brave*, and I started working on how to make these cooperative values come alive in my vision for a new role in the world. But importantly, I also realized that there were communities of people who had been living this way, or attempting to, for decades. I was new to their community, but the community itself was not new.

Wealth inequality is the antithesis of shared prosperity. During the pandemic, the wealth of the world's billionaires grew 54 percent from a combined $8 trillion to just over $12 trillion, while the number of people living in poverty doubled.[1] In the United States, it is not unusual for executive pay to be more than one hundred times that of the median worker, with a handful of companies reporting a 300:1 ratio of executive pay to median pay.[2] Some politicians have suggested a wealth tax on net worth (instead of just income) as one way to address this imbalance.[3] But instead of taxing billionaires to give that money to the government, what if the owners of a business opted to forgo extreme personal wealth in favor of shared prosperity among the larger community of people who make the company prosper? What if they saw themselves as a member of a community and wanted every other member of that community to thrive?

Thankfully, many people all over the world are already living this way or promoting the ideas contained in an integrated life. It is mainstream (white) American culture that has become so divorced from community and is now trying to find its way back. Many others are already there: from community-owned businesses to collective giving circles big and small, many groups are working to advance the principles of an integrated life.

Fortunately, if you know where to look, there are tons of new models of shared ownership and shared prosperity, where people (and their organizations) are fighting to raise the tide for all boats, not just the superyachts. These people are building momentum for rebalancing the fruits of our labors after they have been for too long accumulating primarily to the top 1 percent of wealth holders. I'm excited to introduce you to some of these amazing communities.

Co-ops

You probably hear the word co-op and have some sense of what it means. A co-op (short for "cooperative") is when a group of people band together to negotiate better terms for all of them, whether they are producers (farmers selling milk) or consumers (artists buying supplies). But more than that, co-ops as a legal structure are owned and operated by the members—so the decisions that affect pricing, working conditions, and distribution of profits are decided by what is in the best long-term interests of the members, not what is in the best interests of outside investors trying to maximize profit or extract value.

Some examples of co-ops include credit unions, farmer co-ops like Land O'Lakes, consumer co-ops like REI (the outdoor retailer), and worker-owned cooperatives in many industries, including childcare, farm work, retail, cleaning services, energy, and more. You can find worker-owned co-ops near you using the directory of the US Federation of Worker Cooperatives (https://www.usworker.coop/member-directory).

One global example of a co-op is Mondragon Corporation[4]—a worker-owned cooperative in Spain that employs more than eighty thousand people and includes products and services in finance, retail, industry, and the knowledge economy. They have grown from a single product to a global player in multiple industries. One of the most interesting aspects of their operations is that executive pay cannot exceed a set ratio compared to entry-level pay, such as 5:1 or 8:1.[5]

Mondragon was a cooperative from inception. But some businesses have converted to cooperatives later in their existence. One of the best-known conversions is New Belgium Brewing, which moved from a company with an employee stock ownership plan to a full-on worker-owned cooperative in 2013 and has been managed by worker-owners ever since. (New Belgium Brewing is also a certified B Corp, so you can feel extra good about that Fat Tire ale.) Studies find that worker-owners are more productive and produce more innovation than traditional corporations, as every employee has the pride and motivation of being an owner.

Both co-ops and the employees fare better under these conditions of shared prosperity. The National Center for Employee Ownership (NCEO) found that "companies that have these high-involvement, idea-generating cultures, generate an incremental 6% to 11% added growth per year over what their prior performance relative to their industries would have predicted."[6] Another NCEO report in 2017 "compared workers early in their careers, ages 28 to 34, with employee ownership to their peers without and found being in an ESOP [Employee Stock Ownership Plan] associated with 92% higher median household net wealth, 33% higher median income from wages, and 53% longer median job tenure."[7] As the owners are local, purchasing from a co-op near you has all the benefits of buying from other locally owned businesses, keeping wealth circulating in your community.

To find and join co-ops near you, visit https://identity.coop/ directory, and search for childcare providers, materials and supplies, services, utilities, and, of course, financial institutions like credit unions.

Slow Food

The opposite of fast food, "slow food" as a movement was born in the 1980s out of a protest in Italy on the steps of a proposed McDonald's. It first focused on creating space for leisurely enjoyment of traditional food: "Let us defend ourselves against the universal madness of 'the fast life' with tranquil material pleasure" reads the Slow Food Manifesto.[8] And from the Slow Food International website:

Slow Food was started by Carlo Petrini and a group of activists in the 1980s with the initial aim to defend regional traditions, good food, gastronomic pleasure and a slow pace of life. In over two decades of history, the movement has evolved to embrace a comprehensive approach to food that recognizes the strong connections between plate, planet, people, politics and culture. Today Slow Food represents a global movement involving thousands of projects and millions of people in over 160 countries.[9]

More recently, Slow Food has found a foothold in the United States. With two hundred chapters around the country, Slow Food promotes shared prosperity in the form of campaigns for school gardens, biodiversity, sustainable agriculture, small-scale food production, and more. They promote "slow fish" and "slow meat," focusing on more sustainable methods of production and the conscientious consumption of animal products. Visit the Slow Food USA site (https://slowfoodusa.org) to find recipes, events, and educational materials and join the community of those advocating for "good, clean and fair" food.

If you qualify as an accredited investor, you can find opportunities to make angel investments in Slow Food startups with Sustainable Local Food Investment Group (SLoFIG), by becoming a member at https://slofig.com.

Fair Trade

The fair trade community of producers, advocates, companies, and consumers wants to make it easy to identify items that do right by everyone—the producers and their families, the communities they live in, and our shared planet. They certify goods and services that treat workers and their communities with respect and dignity, rather than exploiting cheap labor and lax environmental protections to sell you a $5 T-shirt. Items that are certified Fair Trade have met rigorous standards for safe working conditions, environmental protection, and sustainable livelihoods.

For some categories of goods, buying Fair Trade–certified products is an important factor because the underlying industries have been particularly exploitive for workers, farmers, and the environment. This includes chocolate, coffee, clothing, and coconut/palm oil. If you want to be sure your purchase isn't violating your values abroad, where you can't see it, check out the Fair Trade USA shopping guides at https://www.fairtradecertified.org/products/shopping-guides (also a great source for gift ideas when you want something to wrap up and present to the guest of honor).

Zebras Unite

Zebras Unite is a movement of entrepreneurs, investors, and allies who focus on building companies that "balance both purpose and profit" (balanced like the stripes of a Zebra).[10] Zebras reject the goal of many venture capitalists to push startups to become "unicorns" (those with a $1 billion or more valuation) and to win at all costs.[11] Zebras Unite describes itself as "a founder-led, cooperatively owned movement creating the culture, capital and community for the next economy."[12]

Zebras are working on "wicked" problems, often with a social component and a strong desire to make the world better through their company. In their 2017 article "Zebras Fix What Unicorns Break," the four women founders (Jennifer Brandel, Mara Zepeda, Astrid Scholz, and Aniyia Williams) call out the problems with the tech startup ecosystem and culture: "A lucky few may profit, but civil society suffers. When shareholder return trumps collective well-being, democracy itself is threatened. The reality is that business models breed behavior, and at scale, that behavior can lead to far-reaching, sometimes destructive outcomes."[13] As an alternative, they are providing a collaborative, participatory community to help grow sustainable companies that create shared prosperity.

If you identify as a Zebra and want to join their community, head to the organization's website, at https://zebrasunite.coop.

Mutual Aid Societies

If we eliminated the idea of charity and "noblesse oblige" (the rich kindly helping the poor), how would people in need have their needs met? One solution is the idea of "mutual aid"—ordinary people helping each other when they need it. In a mutual aid network, we are not separated into classes of givers and receivers, but rather recognize that everyone has something to offer, and everyone has something they need. During 2020, many new mutual aid efforts popped up, organizing volunteers and donations and matching offers with needs via Excel spreadsheets, Facebook groups, Google Docs, and Slack channels, but the idea has been around for centuries longer than our favorite tech tools.

Central to the concept of mutual aid is solidarity, not charity. It's the idea that we stand *together* in the face of obstacles; not that "I am helping you" but that "we are helping each other." Racial justice movements often use similar language, so it's no surprise to learn that mutual aid societies in the United States were first formed among Black communities in the late 1700s, allowing members to pool resources to buy land and start farming, care for the sick and orphaned, and even buy each other's freedom.[14]

When various immigrant groups arrived in America over the next few centuries, they often formed mutual aid societies. Unsupported by government or other citizens, they pooled their resources to create lending circles, help new arrivals learn English, and get jobs.[15]

Today, spurred on by the COVID-19 pandemic, mutual aid societies have proliferated across the United States, from fewer than fifty to more than eight hundred documented efforts. They have expanded from food, clothing, and job assistance to cover mental health services, providing Wi-Fi routers so students can access school remotely, and even vaccine drives to help people make appointments and arrange transportation.[16] Visit Mutual Aid Hub (https://www.mutualaidhub.org) to find and join a mutual aid society near you.

Giving Circles

A giving circle is like the wealthy cousin of a mutual aid society. Instead of helping each other meet their own basic needs, the members of a giving circle pool their discretionary resources to help with community needs. The group will usually pick a small number of charitable organizations to support each year, generally determined via a vote by the members. Giving circles do more than write checks; they often provide members with education on community issues and a space to find others who share their inclination.

Some giving circles are focused on one city or region, but others are organized around another identity. Amplifier (https://www.amplifiergiving.org) is a network of giving circles inspired by Jewish values. With over 120 member circles, they provide tools and resources to start and run an effective giving circle. There are giving circles for African Americans, Asian Americans and Pacific Islanders, and queer youth—but perhaps the most common trait among giving circles is that they are made up largely of women.

One highly visible women's giving circle is Women Moving Millions, which encouraged women of significant means to make bold commitments to advance women and girls. According to research, women are expected to inherit 70 percent of the $41 trillion transferred to the next generation in the coming decades,[17] meaning that "women have an unprecedented opportunity to drive exponential progress toward gender equality."[18] Members pledge to donate $1 million over ten years; as of mid-2021 the movement has 340 members who have committed over $820 million.

At a more local scale, women who can commit $1,000 each year might join a chapter of Impact 100, which, as you might guess, is a group of at least one hundred women who each contribute $1,000 and then decide collectively where the funds go.

Each chapter has its own methodology for selecting charities and divvying up the award dollars, but all emphasize member education and provide varying levels of engagement to suit all schedules and stages of life. Most also have discounts or scholarship programs to help younger members afford to join. Visit the Impact 100 website, at https://impact100global.org, to find a chapter near you, or start a new one!

Social Venture Partners (SVP) is a giving circle with plenty of men and women involved, and their focus is on contributing time and (professional) talents in addition to funding. There are forty SVP chapters around the world, and together they have 3,400 members. In addition to getting an education, SVP members are asked to contribute more than money; their expertise is a key part of the SVP model. Chapters select nonprofit partners and stick with them for three years, providing unrestricted grant dollars while helping with different aspects of operations, finance, impact measurement, and more. Visit the SVP website (https://www.socialventurepartners.org) to see if there is a chapter near you.

You may also find (or start!) a giving circle at your local community foundation, religious institution, or alma mater.

BUILDING AN INTEGRATED LIFE COMMUNITY

Famed entrepreneur and motivational speaker Jim Rohn is believed to have once said, "You are the average of the five people you spend the most time with." So if you want to hang out with other people who are trying to live a more integrated life, come and join our community

continued

at www.theintegratedlife.com. There you will find more practical advice to align everyday choices with your internal compass, opportunities for collective action, encouragement, and affirmation, plus resources and action steps. Have a question? Ask the community. Found a solution or a great resource? Share it with others.

You can also download a printable summary of the seven principles for an integrated life, and sign up for a thirty-day challenge if you want to work on any particular part of your life: food, clothes, cleaning, money, work, celebrations, relationships.

Looking for New Choices

> If you have come here to help me you are wasting your time,
> but if you have come because your liberation is bound up
> with mine, then let us work together.

—LILLA WATSON, 1985 UNITED NATIONS
DECADE FOR WOMEN CONFERENCE

Once a century, during a pandemic, we become laser focused on how much we rely on the goodwill and actions of everyone around us in communities to which we belong, like a neighborhood or a city or a country or a workplace. Of course, this is true all the time, though we often take it for granted. But in times of great crisis, we see with clarity how our well-being is intertwined with others. And how much we all need help from others, including things like wearing a mask properly. Or maintaining six feet of physical distance. Or staying home when we are sick.

But even when there is no disease of the body tearing through our communities, there are often other blights that tear through our communities, poverty chief among them.

When we see poverty and its offspring—crime, homelessness, addiction, incarceration—we have a choice. We can circle the wagons, hoard whatever resources we can, and imagine ourselves to be survivors who are smarter and more adept (more immune?) and simply better than others who have saved less, prepared less, accumulated less. In those circumstances, we tend to place blame for their misfortune on those who were caught unprepared. This is often called a "scarcity mentality," and it's a life full of fear and suspicion and winners and losers.[19] Lots of losers.

But if we are being brave, and honest with ourselves as a society, we would acknowledge how often those growing up in poverty were prevented from preparing by never having a moment's peace, a safe place, a fair chance, or a supportive network to help them thrive. And as a community, we would adopt an "abundance mindset" that says there are enough of all those things for everyone to thrive.

I started writing this book saying, "I'm not trying to save the world; I'm just trying to save myself." But I believe that there are a lot of us out there, and if we bring our lifestyles in line with our desire for shared prosperity, if we vote for the world we want with every purchase—especially the purchases we *don't* make—we can redefine "normal" for a new generation. And maybe, together, we *can* save the world.

Acknowledgments

I first thank the man who made this book possible, Minyoung Sohn, founder of Blue Room Investments, who believed in me and my ability to produce this book before anyone else who isn't related to me. Min's support, along with that of his partner and creative director, Emily Philpott, turned this dream of an integrated life into the book you have now. Min and Emily are using Blue Room as a model of a socially responsible business, and I am proud to be a part of their team as we dream big and have incredible impact.

I thank the many thought partners who have helped me refine and sharpen my ideas over the years, including Maria Kim, Caleb Offley, Banks Benitez, Tracey Stewart, August Ritter, Tobi Becerra, Jesus Salazar, Lindsay Beck, Roweena Naidoo, and too many others to name.

I could never have started and grown a business without the incredible partnership and faith of my business partners and closest friends, Rosalie Sturtevant (my mother) and Sandra Pinter (my big sister).

I am grateful to my first investors, Troy Henikoff and Chuck Templeton; fellow entrepreneurs Neal Sales-Griffin and Chris Conn; and the larger Chicago Techstars family.

Colleagues who have provided moral support also challenged me and helped me find my way, including Stefanie Borsari, Lester Baxter, Michelle Steber, Sarah Cooch, Kim Foreman, Raquel Llanes, Cathy Lund, Lisa Montez, Molly Chafetz, and Lexie Cde Baca.

Notes

Introduction

1. Zack Guzman, "This Simple Tipping Trick Could Save You over $400 a Year," *CNBC*, February 12, 2018, https://www.cnbc.com/2018/02/12/tipping-trick-could-save-you -over-400-a-year.html.

2. Jarkko Levanen, Ville Uusitalo, Anna Harri, Elisa Kareinen, and Lassi Linnanen, "Innovative Recycling or Extended Use? Comparing the Global Warming Potential of Different Ownership and End-of-Life Scenarios for Textiles," *Environmental Research Letters* 16 (2021), https://iopscience.iop.org/article/10.1088/1748-9326/abfac3/pdf.

3. *The Good Place*, season 3, episode 11, "Chidi Sees the Time-Knife," aired January 17, 2019, on NBC.

Chapter 1

1. "The 10 Products You Need for a Stress-Free Move, According to Experts," *CNN*, August 12, 2021, https://trustednews.sumituke.com/the-10-products-you-need-for-a -stress-free-move-according-to-experts-cnn-underscored/.

2. Angela Celebre and Ashley Waggoner Denton, "The Good, the Bad, and the Ugly of the Dove Campaign for Real Beauty," *Inquisitive Mind* 2, no. 19 (2014), https:// www.in-mind.org/article/the-good-the-bad-and-the-ugly-of-the-dove-campaign-for -real-beauty.

3. Audre Lorde, "The Master's Tools Will Never Dismantle the Master's House," in *Sister Outsider: Essays and Speeches* (Berkeley, CA: Crossing Press, 2007), 110.

Chapter 2

1. Tina Fey, *Bossypants* (New York: Reagan Arthur Books, 2011), 84.

2. Gabrielle Bye, "Food Pantries Call for Policy Change, Not Just Donations, to Cure Hunger," *Colorado Times Recorder*, April 5, 2021, https://coloradotimesrecorder .com/2021/04/how-co-food-banks-are-faring.

3. Ilona Lodewijckx, "'Slacktivism': Legitimate Action or Just Lazy Liking?" CitizenLab, May 20, 2020, https://www.citizenlab.co/blog/civic-engagement/slacktivism/.

4. Chris Gayomali, "The Story behind the Gay Marriage Symbol Taking Over Facebook," *The Week*, January 8, 2015, https://theweek.com/articles/466123/story-behind-gay -marriage-symbol-taking-over-facebook.

Chapter 3

1. Paul Keegan, "Here's What Really Happened at That Company That Set a $70,000 Minimum Wage," *Inc.*, November 2015, https://www.inc.com/magazine/201511/paul -keegan/does-more-pay-mean-more-growth.html.

2. Rush Limbaugh, "CEO Buys Short-Term Love," *Rush Limbaugh Show*, April 15, 2015, https://live-rush-limbaugh.pantheonsite.io/daily/2015/04/15/ceo_buys_short_ term_love/.

3. Dan Price, Twitter post, December 11, 2020, https://twitter.com/DanPriceSeattle/ status/1337449625347874817.

4. Dan Price, remarks at Vision 2020 Conference, Great Falls, MT, December 3, 2015.

5. Dan Price, Twitter post, April 26, 2021, https://twitter.com/DanPriceSeattle/ status/1386806718701531141.

6. Bethania Palma, "Are Amazon Workers Forced to Pee in Bottles?" *Snopes*, May 7, 2021, https://www.snopes.com/fact-check/amazon-tweet/.

7. Michael Sainato, "'I'm Not a Robot': Amazon Workers Condemn Unsafe, Grueling Conditions at Warehouse," *The Guardian*, February 5, 2020, https://www.theguardian .com/technology/2020/feb/05/amazon-workers-protest-unsafe-grueling-conditions -warehouse; Food Empowerment Project, "Slaughterhouse Workers," https://foodispower .org/human-labor-slavery/slaughterhouse-workers/ (accessed August 15, 2021).

8. Josh Bivens and Lawrence Mishel, "Understanding the Historic Divergence between Productivity and a Typical Worker's Pay," Economic Policy Institute, September 2, 2015, https://www.epi.org/publication/understanding-the-historic-divergence-between -productivity-and-a-typical-workers-pay-why-it-matters-and-why-its-real/.

9. David Cohen and Brad Feld, "What Is Give First?" Techstars, May 2, 2019, https:// www.techstars.com/the-line/podcasts/what-is-give-first.

Chapter 4

1. For extensive documentation, see the Animal Equity website, at https://animalequality .org, as well as the documentaries *Forks over Knives, Food, Inc., Sick, Fat and Nearly Dead*, and *What the Health?* available on Netflix.

Chapter 5

1. See Longmont Dairy's website, at https://longmontdairy.com.

2. High Plains Food Co-op, "Farmer Gavin's Farm Fresh Eggs," https://shop .highplainsfood.org/Producer/ecf647f9-ebb3-413c-ae9f-39de2b086567 (accessed October 12, 2021).

3. Michael Sainato, "'I'm Not a Robot': Amazon Workers Condemn Unsafe, Grueling Conditions at Warehouse," *The Guardian*, February 5, 2020, https://www .theguardian.com/technology/2020/feb/05/amazon-workers-protest-unsafe-grueling -conditions-warehouse.

4. Civic Economics, "Indie Impact Study Series," http://www.civiceconomics.com/indie -impact.html (accessed November 10, 2021).

Chapter 6

1. "Ecological Footprint," *Wikipedia*, October 13, 2021, https://en.wikipedia.org/wiki/ Ecological_footprint.

2. Earth Overshoot Day, "About Earth Overshoot Day," https://www.overshootday.org/ about-earth-overshoot-day/ (accessed October 12, 2021).

3. "Use It and Lose It: The Outsize Effect of U.S. Consumption on the Environment," *Scientific American*, September 14, 2012, https://www.scientificamerican.com/article/american-consumption-habits/.

4. If you're curious about where you currently stand, visit the Global Footprint Network's footprint calculator, at https://www.footprintcalculator.org, to enter your personal situation and see if your personal footprint consumes more than the earth can produce.

5. "Average Credit Card Debt Statistics," Shift, January 2021, https://shiftprocessing.com/credit-card-debt/.

6. Kimberly Amadeo, "Current US Consumer Debt," *The Balance*, October 12, 2021, https://www.thebalance.com/consumer-debt-statistics-causes-and-impact-3305704.

7. See the biocapacity data on the website of the Global Footprint Network, at https://data.footprintnetwork.org/.

8. Council for Textile Recycling, "The Life Cycle of Secondhand Clothing," http://www.weardonaterecycle.org/about/clothing-life-cycle.html (accessed November 10, 2021).

Chapter 7

1. If you have frequent headaches that aren't solved by living a more integrated life, talk to your dentist! I got rid of 99 percent of my headaches by wearing a guard that aligns my jaw and prevents me from grinding my teeth.

Chapter 8

1. "Why an Apple Today Is Not as Good," *Daily Mail*, https://www.dailymail.co.uk/health/article-207652/Why-apple-today-good.html (accessed October 12, 2021).

2. Environmental Working Group, "Dirty Dozen: EWG's 2021 Shopper's Guide to Pesticides in Produce," https://www.ewg.org/foodnews/dirty-dozen.php (accessed October 12, 2021).

3. Dana Gunders, "Wasted: How America Is Losing Up to 40 Percent of Its Food from Farm to Fork to Landfill," NRDC, August 16, 2017, https://www.nrdc.org/resources/wasted-how-america-losing-40-percent-its-food-farm-fork-landfill.

4. It's not a perfect analysis, but for a take on which chains have the best employee perks, check out Carson Kohler, "Bag a Job at One of These 10 Grocery Stores and Get Some Amazing Benefits," *Penny Hoarder*, March 13, 2017, https://www.thepennyhoarder .com/make-money/grocery-stores-with-employee-perks/.

5. National Restaurant Association, "National Statistics," 2021, https://restaurant.org/ research/restaurant-statistics/restaurant-industry-facts-at-a-glance.

6. For a great explanation of the concept and to search for a CSA near you, visit the LocalHarvest website, at https://www.localharvest.org/csa/.

7. Eliza Barclay, "A Nation of Meat Eaters: See How It All Adds Up," *NPR*, June 27, 2012, https://www.npr.org/sections/thesalt/2012/06/27/155527365/visualizing-a -nation-of-meat-eaters.

8. Johns Hopkins Center for a Livable Future, "Meat Consumption: Trends and Health Implications," https://clf.jhsph.edu/projects/technical-and-scientific-resource-meatless -monday/meatless-monday-resources/meatless-monday-resourcesmeat-consumption -trends-and-health-implications (accessed October 12, 2021).

9. Human Rights Watch, "Worker Health and Safety in the Meat and Poultry Industry," https://www.hrw.org/reports/2005/usa0105/4.htm (accessed October 12, 2021).

10. Leah Douglas, "Mapping Covid-19 Outbreaks in the Food System," *Food and Environment Reporting Network*, April 22, 2020, https://thefern.org/2020/04/mapping -covid-19-in-meat-and-food-processing-plants/.

11. Water Footprint Network, "Water Footprint of Crop and Animal Products: A Comparison," https://waterfootprint.org/en/water-footprint/product-water-footprint/ water-footprint-crop-and-animal-products/ (accessed October 12, 2021).

12. ASPCA, "More Humane Meals, Delivered—Food Delivery Companies Commit to Progressive Animal Welfare Policies," June 10, 2019, https://www.aspca.org/news/ more-humane-meals-delivered-food-delivery-companies-commit-progressive-animal -welfare-policies.

13. Savory, "Land to Market," https://savory.global/land-to-market/ (accessed October 21, 2021).

Chapter 9

1. Council for Textile Recycling, "The Life Cycle of Secondhand Clothing," http://www.weardonaterecycle.org/about/clothing-life-cycle.html (accessed November 10, 2021); Mike Lee, "The Truth about Where Your Donated Clothes End Up," *ABC News*, December 21, 2006, https://abcnews.go.com/WN/truth-donated-clothes-end/story?id=2743456.

2. Elizabeth L. Cline, "The Afterlife of Cheap Clothes," *Slate*, June 18, 2012, https://slate.com/human-interest/2012/06/the-salvation-army-and-goodwill-inside-the-places-your-clothes-go-when-you-donate-them.html.

3. If you want to learn more about the fast fashion industry, I highly recommend the documentary *The True Cost*, available at https://truecostmovie.com/, or the book *Overdressed: The Shockingly High Cost of Cheap Fashion*, by Elizabeth L. Cline.

4. "Australian TV Host Wears Same Suit for a Year and Nobody Notices," *BBC*, November 15, 2014, https://www.bbc.com/news/newsbeat-30069564.

5. World Counts, "It Takes 10,000 Liters of Water to Produce One Kilogram of Cotton," https://www.theworldcounts.com/challenges/consumption/clothing/cotton-farming-water-consumption/story (accessed October 12, 2021).

6. No, really, this terrible idea was an *SNL* skit in 2013: https://www.youtube.com/watch?v=2aVxNH6iN9I.

7. Mitchell P. Jones, "Vegan Leather Made from Mushrooms Could Mould the Future of Sustainable Fashion," *The Conversation*, September 7, 2020, https://theconversation.com/vegan-leather-made-from-mushrooms-could-mould-the-future-of-sustainable-fashion-143988.

8. Geert Peters, "Levi's: Making Water Less Jeans," *The Guardian*, December 20, 2010, https://www.theguardian.com/sustainable-business/levis-water-less-jeans.

Chapter 10

1. Lisa Zamosky, "Is Dirt Good for Kids?" WebMD, September 17, 2014, https://www.webmd.com/parenting/features/kids-and-dirt-germs#1.

2. Sonja Koukel, "Selection and Use of Home Cleaning Products," New Mexico State University, September 2012, https://aces.nmsu.edu/pubs/_g/G304/welcome.html.

3. Environmental Working Group, "Personal Care Products Safety Act Would Improve Cosmetics Safety," https://www.ewg.org/personal-care-products-safety-act-would -improve-cosmetics-safety (accessed October 12, 2021).

4. Oliver Milman, "US Cosmetics Are Full of Chemicals Banned by Europe—Why?" *The Guardian*, May 22, 2019, https://www.theguardian.com/us-news/2019/may/22/ chemicals-in-cosmetics-us-restricted-eu.

5. "How Cosmetics and Skin Care Are Harming the Environment," *Cleure*, September 22, 2020, https://www.cleure.com/blogs/blog/how-cosmetics-and-skin-care-are -harming-the-environment.

6. Environmental Working Group, "Dr. Bronner's Magic Soaps," https://www.ewg.org/ guides/business/421-DrBronnersMagicSoaps/ (accessed October 12, 2021).

Chapter 11

1. Learn more and see how your bank stacks up at the Rainforest Action Network's "Banking on Climate Chaos" page, at https://www.ran.org/bankingonclimatechaos2021.

2. Rodney C., "Banks Make How Much Income from Fees?!" DepositAccounts, https:// www.depositaccounts.com/blog/banks-income-fees.html (accessed October 12, 2021).

3. Matt Egan, "Wells Fargo Wrongly Hit Homebuyers with Fees to Lock In Mortgage Rates," *CNN Business*, October 4, 2017, https://money.cnn.com/2017/10/04/ investing/wells-fargo-mortgage-rate-lock-fees/index.html.

4. Matt Egan, "Wells Fargo Can't Seem to Escape Its Troubled Past," *CNN Business*, January 15, 2021, https://www.cnn.com/2021/01/15/investing/wells-fargo-bank -earnings-scandal/index.html.

5. Board of Governors of the Federal Reserve System, "Community Reinvestment Act (CRA)," September 28, 2020, https://www.federalreserve.gov/consumerscommunities/ cra_about.htm.

6. Anna Kusmer, "Climate Divestment Activists Draw Inspiration from South Africa's Anti-Apartheid Struggle," *The World*, March 18, 2021, https://www.pri.org/ stories/2021-03-18/climate-divestment-activists-draw-inspiration-south-africa-s -anti-apartheid.

7. Rockefeller Brothers Fund, "Fossil Fuel Divestment," https://www.rbf.org/mission-aligned-investing/fossil-fuel-divestment (accessed October 12, 2021).

8. Emma Whitford, "Divestment Gap Emerges," *Inside Higher Ed*, April 28, 2021, https://www.insidehighered.com/news/2021/04/28/divestment-gains-some-colleges-can-it-spread-where-oil-rules.

9. Anemona Hartcollis, "Harvard Says It Will Not Invest in Fossil Fuels," *New York Times*, September 10, 2021, https://www.nytimes.com/2021/09/10/us/harvard-divestment-fossil-fuels.html.

Chapter 12

1. Urban Institute, "The Nonprofit Sector in Brief, 2019," June 4, 2020, https://nccs.urban.org/publication/nonprofit-sector-brief-2019; National Council of Nonprofits, "Downloadable Charts and Figures," https://www.nonprofitimpactmatters.org/data/downloadable-charts (accessed October 12, 2021).

2. Giving USA, *Giving USA, 2021: The Annual Report on Philanthropy for the Year 2020* (Chicago: Giving USA, 2021).

3. Jeffrey M. Jones, "Percentage of Americans Donating to Charity at New Low," *Gallup*, May 14, 2020, https://news.gallup.com/poll/310880/percentage-americans-donating-charity-new-low.aspx.

4. Dan Pallotta, "Stop Giving Donors What You Think They Want," *Harvard Business Review*, February 15, 2011, http://blogs.hbr.org/pallotta/2011/02/stop-giving-donors-what-you-th.html.

5. "U.S. Missionaries Charged with Kidnapping in Haiti," *CNN*, February 5, 2010, http://www.cnn.com/2010/CRIME/02/04/haiti.arrests/index.html.

6. Deacon Patrick Moynihan, "T-Shirt Mistakes," *Catholic News Agency*, February 10, 2012, https://www.catholicnewsagency.com/column/52028/t-shirt-mistakes; Sasha Alyson, "I Was Supposed to Get Life-Changing Aid but All I Got Was This Lousy T-Shirt," *Karma Colonialism*, https://karmacolonialism.org/world-vision-passes-out-losing-team-tshirts/ (accessed October 24, 2021).

7. Jesse Bogan, "Nonprofit Accused of Making False Claims," *St. Louis Post-Dispatch*, July 30, 2010, https://www.stltoday.com/news/state-and-regional/missouri/nonprofit-accused-of-making-false-claims/article_e8da27b1-2244-54ec-a3fc-a68ab91b4060.html; Aimee Levitt, "Domestic Violence Center Shut Down for Being a Total Fraud," *Riverfront Times*, July 29, 2010, https://www.riverfronttimes.com/newsblog/2010/07/29/domestic-violence-center-shut-down-for-being-a-total-fraud.

8. Blue Avocado, "The Economy, Bad Decisions, and Nonprofits," October 15, 2008, https://blueavocado.org/none-yet/the-economy-bad-decisions-and-nonprofits-10-15-08/.

9. Lucy Bernholz, "Buzzword #6—Embedded Giving," *Philanthropy 2173*, November 3, 2007, https://philanthropy.blogspot.com/2007/11/buzzword-6-embedded-giving.html.

Chapter 13

1. Cone, "2019 Porter Novelli/Cone Gen Z Purpose Study," https://www.conecomm.com/research-blog/cone-gen-z-purpose-study (accessed October 13, 2021).

2. Shawn Achor, Andrew Reece, Gabriella Rosen Kellerman, and Alexi Robichaux, "9 out of 10 People Are Willing to Earn Less Money to Do More-Meaningful Work," *Harvard Business Review*, November 6, 2018, https://hbr.org/2018/11/9-out-of-10-people-are-willing-to-earn-less-money-to-do-more-meaningful-work.

3. Andrea Hsu, "As the Pandemic Recedes, Millions of Workers Are Saying 'I Quit,'" *NPR*, June 24, 2021, https://www.npr.org/2021/06/24/1007914455/as-the-pandemic-recedes-millions-of-workers-are-saying-i-quit.

4. Certified B Corporation, "Certification," https://bcorporation.net/certification (accessed October 3, 2021).

5. A. R. Sorkin, "Ex-Corporate Lawyer's Idea: Rein In 'Sociopaths' in the Boardroom," *New York Times*, September 4, 2021, https://www.nytimes.com/2019/07/29/business/dealbook/corporate-governance-reform-ethics.html.

6. J. Gamble, "The Most Important Problem in the World," *Medium*, September 4, 2021, https://medium.com/@jgg4553542/the-most-important-problem-in-the-world-ad22ade0ccfe.

7. Each state establishes rules for corporations formed under its own laws. Visit B Lab, at https://benefitcorp.net, to see what the status is in your state.

8. Impact Opportunity, "About Us," https://impactopportunity.org/about-us/ (accessed November 10, 2021).

9. Net Impact, "About Net Impact," https://netimpact.org/about (accessed October 26, 2021).

10. Edelman, "2018 Edelman Trust Barometer," January 21, 2018, https://www.edelman.com/trust/2018-trust-barometer.

11. Porter Novelli, "Feeling Purpose: 2019 Porter Novelli/Cone Purpose Biometrics Study," May 28, 2019, https://www.porternovelli.com/findings/2019-porter-novelli-cone-purpose-biometrics-study-feeling-purpose/.

Chapter 15

1. Logan Ury, "Want to Improve Your Relationship? Start Paying More Attention to Bids," Gottman Institute, February 11, 2019, https://www.gottman.com/blog/want-to-improve-your-relationship-start-paying-more-attention-to-bids/.

2. M. Blazoned, "The Default Parent," *Huff Post*, December 6, 2017, https://www.huffpost.com/entry/the-default-parent_b_6031128.

3. Francesca Donner, "The Household Work Men and Women Do, and Why," *New York Times*, February 12, 2020, https://www.nytimes.com/2020/02/12/us/the-household-work-men-and-women-do-and-why.html.

4. Claire Cain Miller, "Young Men Embrace Gender Equality, but They Still Don't Vacuum," *New York Times*, February 11, 2020, https://www.nytimes.com/2020/02/11/upshot/gender-roles-housework.html.

5. Claire Cain Miller, "How Same-Sex Couples Divide Chores, and What It Reveals about Modern Parenting," *New York Times*, May 16, 2018, https://www.nytimes.com/2018/05/16/upshot/same-sex-couples-divide-chores-much-more-evenly-until-they-become-parents.html.

6. Shelley J. Correll, Stephen Benard, and In Paik, "Getting a Job: Is There a Motherhood Penalty?" *American Journal of Sociology* 112, no. 5 (2007): 1297–1339.

7. "Fred Rogers: Look for the Helpers," *YouTube*, April 15, 2013, https://www.youtube.com/watch?v=-LGHtc_D328.

Chapter 16

1. Aimee Picchi, "Billionaires Got 54% Richer during Pandemic, Sparking Calls for 'Wealth Tax,'" *CBS News*, March 31, 2021, https://www.cbsnews.com/news/billionaire -wealth-covid-pandemic-12-trillion-jeff-bezos-wealth-tax/.

2. PayScale, "CEO Pay: How Much Do CEOs Make Compared to Their Employees?" https://www.payscale.com/data-packages/ceo-pay/full-list (accessed October 13, 2021).

3. Warren Democrats, "Ultra-Millionaire Tax," https://elizabethwarren.com/plans/ultra -millionaire-tax (accessed October 13, 2021).

4. Mondragon, "About Us," https://www.mondragon-corporation.com/en/about-us/ (accessed October 13, 2021).

5. "Mondragon Corporation," *Wikipedia*, September 25, 2021, https://en.wikipedia.org/ wiki/Mondragon_Corporation.

6. National Center for Employee Ownership, "What Is Ownership Culture?" https:// www.nceo.org/ownership-culture (accessed October 13, 2021).

7. National Center for Employee Ownership, "Research on Employee Ownership," https://www.nceo.org/employee-ownership-data/academic-research (accessed October 13, 2021).

8. Slow Food, "Slow Food Manifesto," https://slowfood.com/filemanager/Convivium%20 Leader%20Area/Manifesto_ENG.pdf (accessed October 13, 2021).

9. Slow Food, "Our History," https://www.slowfood.com/about-us/our-history/ (accessed October 13, 2021).

10. Zebras Unite, "The Zebras Unite Community," https://zebrasunite.mn.co/ (accessed October 13, 2021).

11. Zebras Unite, "Our Vision," https://zebrasunite.coop/our-vision (accessed October 27, 2021).

12. See the Zebras Unite home page, at https://zebrasunite.coop.

13. Jennifer Brandel, Mara Zepeda, Astrid Scholz, and Aniyia Williams, "Zebras Fix What Unicorns Break," *Medium*, March 8, 2017, https://medium.com/zebras-unite/zebrasfix -c467e55f9d96.

14. Christine Fernando, "Mutual Aid Networks Find Roots in Communities of Color," *AP News*, January 21, 2021, https://apnews.com/article/immigration-coronavirus-pandemic -7b1d14f25ab717c2a29ceafd40364b6e.

15. Jassmin Poyaoan, "How Lending Circles and Mutual Aid Groups Create Community Resilience," *Resilience*, August 26, 2013, https://www.resilience.org/stories/2013-08-26/ how-lending-circles-mutual-aid-groups-create-community-resilience/.

16. Kimiko de Freytas-Tamura, "How Neighborhood Groups Are Stepping In Where the Government Didn't," *New York Times*, March 3, 2021, https://www.nytimes .com/2021/03/03/nyregion/covid-19-mutual-aid-nyc.html.

17. Bruce DeBoskey, "Women's Voices Ring Clear in Philanthropic World," *WealthManagment*, June 19, 2017, https://www.wealthmanagement.com/philanthropy/ women-s-voices-ring-clear-philanthropic-world.

18. Women Moving Millions, "Join Our Community," https://womenmovingmillions.org/ community/ (accessed October 13, 2021).

19. Stephen R. Covey, *The 7 Habits of Highly Effective People: Powerful Lessons in Personal Change* (New York: Simon and Schuster, 2013), 230.

About the Author

SHARON SCHNEIDER is an entrepreneur, a philanthropy expert, an impact investor, and a strategist who advises socially conscious founders and family offices. She has overseen more than $1.5 billion in philanthropic capital deployed through grants, impact investments, advocacy efforts, and business operations from some of the world's most prominent families, including members of the Giving Pledge, the Forbes 400 wealthiest individuals, top-ten US private foundations, and others.